When You Can't Scream...
Or 10 Reasons Why I Smoke

When You Can't Scream...
Or 10 Reasons Why I Smoke

Doren Damico

DreamingD Enterprises

www.dorendamico.com

Low Definition Edition
Printed by CreateSpace
www.CreateSpace.com/6354767

ISBN-10 0692743650
ISBN-13 978-0692743652

Cover Photograph Credit: Judith Foster Thompson

Title Page Photograph Credit: Vicente O. Arellano

A Beginning to the End Photograph Credit: Violet Soto*

All Other Photographs Credit: Judith Foster Thompson

Creative Director of Photographs: Doren Damico

Photo Editors: Doren Damico, Philip Ruiz, Violet Soto, and Ana Rosa

Autobiographical Narrative Editor: Michael Ray De Los Angeles

Interior and Cover Design: Doren Damico and Violet Soto

* 3 Additional Bio Photos Credit: Violet Soto

Disclaimer:
Warning: There are growing indications regarding the mediating benefits of smoking for some citizens. However, research is on select high-risk groups. While personal anecdotal evidence is that smoking may have kept me alive, I do not recommend its use. Smoking is addictive and bad for your health. In fact, my best advice is never pick up a cigarette. Go snowboarding

Doren Damico

This book is dedicated
To those who pause in strange and normal places.
Thank you for sharing the joy of lighting up in a stiff wind,
And sparing a cigarette when it was most needed.
Remember, there are always
Surprises by the wayside.

When You Can't Scream...

Poetry and Photographs

Or 10 Reasons Why I Smoke

Autobiographical Narrative

The Lady Sings

When You Can't Scream...
Or 10 Reasons Why I Smoke

Unfolding From The Dark

I wrote this book with the title as a seed: *When You Can't Scream, Or 10 Reasons Why I Smoke.* Once I had the title, I wrote over twenty poems to evoke the mood of my screams, silenced by cigarettes. This is a collection of true events, to include the screaming trauma of multiple rapes and the reflective silences of my inner world. I hope it illuminates my choice to smoke. I know there are no guarantees for sympathy, except perhaps, what I offer myself. Through this book, I am a voice of complex understanding and compassion. I am sunlight on my own field of flowers.

This seed was incubated in the darkness of silence and abandonment, scalded in the trauma of rape, and nurtured through art. Poetry speaks of all conditions, material and spiritual. Poetry screams from my voice, through the reader's voice, through time. It takes the twisty lyrical path of my insides, and peeling me inside out, the seed breaks open and new life sprouts, reaching for the light.

Words are powerful and yet much of my life has been veiled by things unspoken. I decided to add photographs to this project to capture my intimate feelings in visual form. I solicited the collaboration of photographers and models and embarked on learning how to plan and direct photo shoots that met my objectives. As this is a woman's story, the models are all women of varying ages, ethnicities and body types. These images may open eyes in ways that words cannot.

Eventually I was encouraged to share my biographical relationship to cigarettes more openly and honestly through a personal narrative. I also wanted to make an effort to mediate the negative implications of a book focused on smoking. To that effect I've inserted throughout the narrative, research-based information about the dangers of smoking, cigarettes and the brain, the tobacco industry and varied perspectives on mental and emotional wellness, as well as information about quitting smoking.

I think every creative project is a kind of childbirth. And what I set out to do when I began, has become so much more than I planned. Like a child, at first a holy captivating, troublesome thing, this project grew, claimed its own life and personality. It is still becoming, unfolding from the dark depths of pain into the brilliant beauty of sunshine and flowers. I scream because I need to be heard. I write to share and to heal myself of the dissociative tendencies my smoking implies. This will be the fruit of my endeavor.

Cigarettes in the Rain

I want you to know
So you will no longer be
Innocent
Ignorant
Hypocrites

Like cigarettes
In the rain
Smoking will kill ya
Worst of all the stigmata
Drop the nails
From your eyes
To the earth
Let them stay
Let them rust

I want you to know
I've spent my life
In an off-again on-again
Love affair
With a cigarette
Even knowing
What I know

Now ask yourself why
Don't answer
Just ask
And wonder
At holy smoke and tears
Now listen
To cigarettes in the rain

Delicate Flower Dying Slowly

You were my first and my last breath
Stolen from my mother's
Cigarette purse
Hiding on the side of the house
Delicate flower dying slowly
Inhaling with curiosity
Exhaling with purpose
The first
Cigarette Number One
I took you to stop the nightmares
I took you to stop the voices
I took you to run away

I am like a faithful dog
I take you in my mouth
Again and again
My ears hear the keening
Of countless voices
The world-song wailing
For everyone dying
The joyous sound of hope
For everyone born
Do you hear it?
Death
Change
Sunrise

I take you to bear the nightmares
I take you to bear the voices
For just a moment
Crouching low
A flower
Among the shadows
I take you to bear the day

You will be my ritual incense
Modern temple-market sacrifice
Trembling among my brethren
Keeping my promises
Knowing what I postponed
For years
With every smoke
For dying later

Thrill-seeker inhaling with curiosity
Rebel exhaling with purpose

I will survive the nightmares
With every smoke
For bearing more
I will survive the voices
With every smoke
A death wish stay
I will survive waiting
With every smoke
Delicate flower dying slowly
From first breath
Until this last

A Bright Sharp Tool

l am a bright sharp tool
l am awake and aware that l am awake
Seeing how right and left
Here and there
Then and now
Whatever turn l take
l am swift in the hands
Of those who would use me
l am sharp and cutting
When passion moves me
l am sometimes frightened
By myself

You are mistaken
If you think love
Will not chop off the foot to save the soul
l am in the making of new ways
The destruction of old days
The building of roads and bridges
Setting itches in the brain
So you blame me, curse me
For stoking the fires of your pain
This is my gift
Crashing and splintering
Carving and sculpting
Have you ever cut a road
Through a mountain?
None other than what l was crafted
In their hands l have been hefted

l will speak truth
l will speak justice
And you will shun me
l will champion the weak
And speak
To the lies in the room
The father, the son, the holy spirit
The mother, the daughter, the holy soul

Guide my bright edges
Help me cool and dim
The sparks of friction
For the day is obscured
And l have been buffeted right and left
By ghosts that love to catch my ear
By angels eagerly bound for my services
By families, loved ones, and higher selves
Calling the forces of my will
Like channeling the wind
You call me
But you cannot control my nature
Nor shall l

Misunderstood
It pains me to cut you sharply and you shout
Misunderstood
It pains me to be the mirror
That blinds you in the sun
l cry out silently, unheard
For it to stop
For you to heal from your gangrene
For you to see what l have only reflected
You think l am unaffected
But l am caught
In the hands of your shining karma

Roll down the windows of the car now
I'm lightin' up a cigarette
Lettin' just a little bit
Of my spirit go free
On the smoke
Then it's back to work
Being blamed for the edges of my creations
A spiral blade of illumination
A bright sharp tool
In the hands of love

A Volcano Once Dormant

I realize everywhere
Nowhere, nowhen, nohow
Am I free
If I could tell you all my visions
Tell you what I see
I can't
I rein myself in
With a cigarette

Oh humans!
I tire so easily
From the patterns of your lies
Cracked and dirty tombs
Choking off the power of my speech
Preventing me from leaping ahead
Into the beautiful moments with you

I am a wish
Waiting to explode
To multiply and manifest
At your behest
Against oppositions
Three times
Three wishes
Then I am done

Wish one
A culture will come
Where those like me walk free
And the raging emotional fires
That live in we, the people
Free, like the youngest of children

Changeable
Forgiving
Prone to laughter
We fall and get right back up to run
We hate
Then learn in a flash
So many reasons to love
Our lava tears
A vicious tongue
Anger, joy
Uncontained

Wish two you
Will accept our screams
In the most loving way
As a human way
To adjust and relate
To extreme sensations
Injustice rumbling in all the nations
We cry out in exaltation
Screaming freely everywhere
All for you, foul society
Deaf to our tectonics
Denying metamorphosis
Do not cover your ears
But diving
Striving
Sacrificing
Discover our violent song

Wish three I see
In the far to come and not today

(continued)

There will be a place for me
Cascading
Ricocheting
Dance
And I shall sing
Multiplying
True combining
Symphony of elation
Pain in transformation
Defying
Gravity
Time
Space
My screaming creations
Birthing Islands
Somewhere
Somewhen
Somehow

But that one day
Is not mine, not now

I reach
For a cigarette
My friends
Are not ready yet
My conspicuous multiplications
Are currently fading striations
A volcano once dormant
Now smoking
Wishing for release
A scream becoming
That once erupting
Must lay waste
Ash and gray
I rein myself in
With a cigarette
Everywhere
I am silent

A Cigarette at the Edge of the World

If I could scream at any necessary time
Or go hunting for days
I would smoke much less
Perhaps not at all

Even orgasms have to be constrained
Maybe this should be a list
About why I could spend the rest of my life
On some secluded mountain
Where I can scream, fuck, and smoke all I want

But it would be cold in winter
I'd miss the art of TV
The thrill of helium balloons
And tango dancing

So I drive out to the sea
And take long inhales on a cigarette
No screaming orgasms
Just a cigarette at the edge of the world

Alas, I Ramble

Alas, I ramble
In the long ago and far away
In the not today and soon to come
Forgive me
The story meanders
For you
Leaps across chasms
Swims in hopelessness
For me
Dying
At once and at last
Is like meeting a lost love

Alas, I ramble
A dizzy telling
Of time unraveling
Scarred hands untangling
I lie not to hide the truth
To preserve it
Send it through time
Change is what comes
For the long ago is changeless
But you knot the soon to come
As if it were a wild horse to be broken
Not a gift to be savored
And I sit unwinding
A moment

Alas, I ramble
For the story
Feels irrelevant
A winter garden grows
On the horizon dies
This lazy afternoon of youth
Rushed and scurrying
Have you no time?
To breathe?
To play?
"Alas, no," you tell me.
"I am no longer a child."
So I laugh and reply:
"A half a cigarette stub
With enough for a quick smoke,
Should not be discarded so easily."

In Tile and Glass Cages

This one makes me think of sex
And then forget again
Being raped in a bathroom
So it's the cigarette
I might want after great sex
And it's the cigarette
I smoke to forget rape sex
I still can't scream
I'm still trapped
In tile and glass cages

That's when you think of a cigarette
And then when you are here
Wherever you are
Catching those slow, deep
Poisonous breaths
You aren't there
Where your whole life
Was taken away from you
'Cause you have to spend
The rest of your life using restrooms
Restrooms where there is no rest
Cigarette Number Six is for this
And for after the shower
That will never cleanse
Contaminated brain cells
You get through that hell
Again

To the other side
And breathe
And maybe cry a little
Because you still can't remember
What happened in the end

In that big black void
You know you forgot
'Cause it was real bad
You light up a cigarette
You have a smoke
And a good cry
Or not
Just cold numb nothingness
Nothing but a cigarette
So good in the rain
To remind you that you are alive
You are breathing
And the rain falls for you
For all the tears you can cry
Or can't cry
Trying to cry away those memories
Corrupted interrupted amygdala dendrites
And how they painted the rest of your life
In tile and glass cages
Where no one can hear you
Even if you do scream

A Pause on the Avalanche of Life

Not just any moment
The one when you feel heaven
Fall out from under your wings
Sharp aloneness
Permeates your being
Every conversation
High tech coliseum
Pause that white noise thought

You walk outside
Into the frigid crisp snow
Gloves off
You light a cigarette
Put your hands in your pockets
And watch the wind whip up ashes
Contemplating the mountains
The distance against a grey sky

In the raw, red-nosed now
Of needled air and white
In the imminence like silence
Anticipation of a spring day
You see clearly
You've been fooling yourself
You thought you were in heaven
Maybe for a moment you were

Then you discover your life
That let down plummet from sky
Wakeup to reality and face truth
Aloneness is....not bad
It's just painful
To open your eyes
In the frozen wind and smoke
To see the avalanche coming

So you close them
Puff on your cigarette
Stamp your feet
Let the chemicals take effect
For just a moment
Forget
Voluminous certainty
Boomerang death

Truth catches the breath
Great roiling terror engulfs
Brave silent screaming
I am called to my maker
Unlike you
I return awake and again to these lives
Remembering who I am
Until the end of Earth's existence

(continued)

Once and a thousand times for me
The avalanche comes
For my children's children's children
Through epochs of mutation
Until we feed upon water and sunlight
Unrecognized
Unbelieving
That great white wave

There is no stopping it
Cry and beg on your knees
There is no warning
Almost, face justice
With a smile
Set your back
To cold raging
Light a last cigarette
Pause before death
Remember this day

Smoking in the snow
Hunched shoulders and shivers
Outside the party
Your love
This once in a thousand lives
Just on the other side of the door
Open your eyes
Watch smoke dance in the wind

Not just any moment
A pause on the avalanche of life
One more breath
The only one who knows
An avalanche is coming
And all the cigarettes in the world
Can't stop it

Lipstick Stained

Wake me
Deadly glorious lightning storm
A thousand words
Before thunder
A hundred words
Shaking my windows
Ten bells in the dark
Nine cigarettes
Smoldering in the pool hall parking lot
Outrageous laughter

I'm dreaming
Caustic burning war zone
A thousand bullets
Before midnight
A hundred bullets
Tolling my sorrows
Eight steps to the phone
Seven glasses of wine
Salted in seaside mist
Compassion and friendship

Wake me
Radical furious salsa liaisons
A thousand songs
Before morning
A hundred songs
Matching my tempos
Six glorious years
Five minutes of screaming
Honeyed in sunrise bliss
Inevitable embrace

I'm dreaming
Frantic courageous frozen lips
A thousand kisses
Before submission
A hundred kisses
Erasing tomorrow
Four breaths deep and raging
Three times I shout your name
Hallowed in fresh tears
Desperate and daring

Wake me
Spurious mechanical mundane terror
A thousand heartbeats
Before goodbye
A hundred heartbeats
Echoing your soul
Two steps to the phone
One
Incandescent light
Lipstick stained cigarette
Glowing and discarded

Wanderers by the Wayside

Wanderers
By the wayside
You beg a spare cigarette
Sharing a match
Warm concrete walls

Watching
By the river
Resting our hands
On cool grassy spines
While we pass the torch

Listening
By the backdoor
We meet in the rain
Ignoring the time
Dirt under our nails
Tear impaled smoke rings

Laughing
By the moonlight
We ponder God
Arguing over Her name
Serenade of crickets
Thick indrawn pauses

Speaking
By the fire
We muse and wonder
Where the river starts
Why the world
Asks for nothing

You tell me your name
Bonding surprises
By the wayside
We find each other
Strangers no more

10 Places To Go Scream

By this time
I'm making myself sick
A slow death or dying now
That's the trick
And I'm contemplating a list
Of ten ways to die

Break that chain of thought
And switch
Switch, dammit
Switch
I stamp my foot
The right foot
And tell myself to switch again

Death on the brain
Is a hard act to follow
No manner of pleading
Crying, believing, or trying
Will get me off this train
Only dying

So I smoke a cigarette
Another
Finally
I decide to write a list titled:
10 Places to Go Scream

It is a leaping off the cliff
The cliff of my insanity
A landing on the page
A tumbling release
A brave embrace
A separation
Of fact and fiction
The cigarette
The chemical stain
Dripping through me
Substitute for my blood
I get my pen
And this is it
In one fell slash

10 Places to Go Scream:

#1 A windy
Abandoned beach at night
My screams crashing
A world's tears falling
Mightily down my cheeks

#2 A high mountain forest
Quiet of new snow
Tear that scream out of silence
Waking hungry bears

(continued)

#3 Under the freeway
A roaring raging hit song lost
In my spinning traffic
Heart breakdown

#4 In a vast cave
Dark
Vaulting shelters
Empty
High-rise streets
Great
Cold stone spaces
Alone
I sing and scream for hours
As If
I am the only one left
And no one can listen

#5 At the zoo
In a cage
With the wild
Domesticated
Saves slash slaves
Of exquisite
Not yet extinct
Creatures

I howl and scream
When the animals roar
Trumpet
Hiss and call
Across the walls
And fences
Screaming into every corner
Of my disproportionate world

#6 In the flames of fighting mean
Or a terrible injustice
In real flames
Or the flames of war
I have screamed
In all those infernos before

#7 In the hospital
In pain
Abandoned
Torn from the womb
Having the womb torn from me
One day dying
I have and will scream there

(continued)

#8 On a crazy thrill ride
Like a roller coaster
Or life
All colorful gasps
And insane laughter
With a stiff neck
And a raw throat later
To remember the journey

9 To a new lifetime's
Baby body
When l reincarnate
l'm going to scream
As much as l feel
Like screaming
Fill my little lungs
With air
And the fire of life
Of hunger
Of pain
Of ecstasy
They will say
l am a troublesome
Colicky baby
They won't even guess
l'm making up
For a lifetime
Of silence

10 lf you die
Before l can
l will scream beyond telling
The neighborhood
Will tremble
At the depths of my grief
l will go on
Screaming inside
For a good long while
To remember
The great heights
Of our ecstasy
To forget
The moments
When you wounded me
To release
Your spirit
From any debt
To know my pain

Then
After all that screaming
lf l'm still alive in the end
l'll probably light
Cigarette # Ten

Last Cigarettes

One of my favorite movies
Quit smoking mini-plots
The Fifth Element
A row of cigarettes
A glass wall dispenser
Orange filters
White paper
Each cigarette
Gets shorter and shorter
Where are the cigarettes
In The Matrix?
Sarah Connor smoking
In black tank
Jumper boots and army pants
A knife in one hand
Sunglasses on
A cigarette in the other

Who is the Terminator?
The cigarette and the writer
Butts all foul lumped
In stinking glass ashtrays
Stranger Than Fiction
Standing on the precipice
Pages flying
True Romance
Gunfire and feathers
A bloodied lip
The slick flick of a silver lighter
Blade Runner style
Bright flame and eyelashes
Last cigarettes
Constantine
Finally quits

Autobiographical Narrative

Lung Cancer and Black Calm

"I've spent my life in an off-again on-again love affair with a cigarette, even knowing what I know."

— *Cigarettes in the Rain*

Of course I know that smoking is dangerous! On a recent visit to the doctor, I calculated that despite my numerous periods of being smoke free, I've smoked cigarettes cumulatively for over two decades.

Why have I allowed myself to harm myself in such a way? Is it addiction? A lack of discipline? Is the tobacco industry to blame? Or my mother, whose love I yearned for, whose cigarette I first stole?

I believe it is a complex organism, my love affair with smoking. Smoking being the symptom of a much greater culprit: growing up as a hyper-Empath in a riotous world. If anything, I blame stress and trauma. I blame the way my brain was altered by smoking at a very young age. Tobacco became a strategic tool to stimulate the calming pleasures of dopamine in my brain when the world filled me with terror and aching, when I needed to rage at injustice but was taught that my rage could change nothing.

"A madhouse!" I shout silently to our creator, to the universe, or both.

So much in this world should be celebrated with screaming: hunger, accomplishment, how comedy overcomes misery, pain, injustice, orgasms, the dominoes of misunderstanding, the miraculous and painful birth of a child...death. Yet, like all good, and proper domesticated humans, I've learned we are supposed to scream only for the runners in a race, the rock star and his guitar...for winning...Ra! Ra! Rah! How is it that these screams are welcomed, yet my screams for justice are shunned, silenced, and sequestered by society?

According to the Centers for Disease Control, cigarette smoking harms nearly every organ of the body and affects a person's overall health. It causes many diseases to include coronary heart disease, stroke and lung cancer. Smoking can also cause cancer almost anywhere in the body! Even if a smoker doesn't get lung cancer, smoking will have a deleterious effect on the lungs and leads directly to COPD (Chronic Obstructive Pulmonary Disease), emphysema, chronic bronchitis, and sometimes, asthma. Smoking also makes it harder for women to become pregnant, it affects the health of teeth and gums, can cause tooth loss, increases the risk of cataracts, affects night vision, is a cause of type 2 diabetes, increases inflammation and decreases immune function.[1]

I haven't been diagnosed with lung cancer, but I often imagine that lung cancer will be the cause of my death. Even if I quit smoking for good, I have an increased risk of developing lung cancer. It is both an invading anxiety and a fantastical drama, the first act, featuring an enchanting meeting between the cigarette and I. The last act will be my death, like drowning, except much more slowly. The once black calm will pull me down into a gurgling panicked struggle for breath.

I don't even let myself think about throat or mouth cancer. I've seen the photographs and watched the morbid anti-smoking commercials. As a singer and poet, throat or mouth cancer would be a cruel irony!

Meanwhile, I smoke. And I want you to know: Sometimes, it feels like smoking keeps me alive. That's not to say I haven't tried other methods of coping with the world and learning to relax; good works, meditation, singing, listening to calming music, walking, dancing, coloring, sex, food, medicine, prayer and writing have all been avenues of survival. Yet none of these are so quick, so sure a way of calming the tidal wave before it overwhelms me in screaming.

I want you to know: Cigarettes have helped me to cope with poverty, injustice, domestic violence, a lifetime of stress and numerous rapes; I've used cigarettes to survive, they've helped me hold back the screams towards a society that doesn't welcome my discontent, and helped me to continue to live in the madhouse I couldn't change.

Now, how silently the screams still echo and rage in the cave of my soul, while the smoke bathes my brain, my throat, my blood, my heart and my lungs in black calm.

So what is the function or service of this art? Well, I did it for compassion's sake, as a way to process my screams, to love and understand myself. I did it to continue in a world where what I can change, being so little, must somehow be enough. I want to explain the hidden wounds that are made visible by the cigarette my hand brings to my lips. I want to share the love and learning I've discovered along the way.

I have colorful, happy stories, good memories to write about. I believe whole-heartedly that love is the ultimate purpose of life, even of suffering. But in this work, I aim to illuminate in black, white and gray.

I do not intend to glorify or glamorize smoking through my poetry or photographs. I'm not using trauma as an excuse for self-sabotaging behaviors; furthermore, I would not suggest that people start smoking. Rather, I want to share a part of my story, with the hope that readers' minds and hearts will contemplate the habit of smoking through a different lens. Perhaps, the apathy that arises when we judge others' habits, can be replaced by empathy for the life struggles we share.

However, this narrative describes how I started smoking and how I use smoking to cope. It explains the effects of cigarettes on the brain, and alludes to certain groups of people that mediate life's challenges with cigarettes. Indeed, I honor and support non-smoking efforts that produce health and healing. As I write this, I hope to quit smoking soon, even knowing that for me, and perhaps for those around me, there is a definite price. To that effect, you will find at the conclusion of this narrative, links to organizations and methods that support people to quit smoking.

1. *"Health Effects." Centers for Disease Control and Prevention. Centers for Disease Control and Prevention, 1 Oct. 2015. Web. May 2016. Content Source: Office on Smok-ing and Health, National Center for Chronic Disease Prevention and Health Promotion <http://www.cdc.gov/tobacco/data_statistics/fact_sheets/health_effects/effects_cig_smoking/>*

When You Can't Scream...Or 10 Reasons Why I Smoke

First Breath, First Screams, First Cigarette

"You were my first and last breath, stolen from my mother's cigarette purse."

— Delicate Flower Dying Slowly

I came into this world screaming. My birth was a difficult and long labor after a difficult and extended pregnancy: I imagine that I was a prescient fetus, knowing full well the kinds of suffering I'd experience in this life, and I did not want to leave the sanctuary of my mother's womb.

As a babe, I screamed when I hungered for breast milk and skin-to-skin caress. But my mother did not breastfeed me. She went back to work quite soon to support my three year-old brother, her new daughter, and my father who was attending law school.

I've come to understand the incredible value of breastfeeding, and how that lack in my childhood, negatively impacted my own resilience. Not only does breastfeeding provide nutrients and immunity specifically catered to an individual baby's needs, it provides significant amounts of the "love" hormone, oxytocin. Each time a mother breastfeeds, she releases this powerful hormone. Oxytocin decreases heart rate and blood pressure and has a calming effect on both mother and child. Additionally, the positive benefits of oxytocin last long after the nursing relationship ends. It has been proven to reduce the severity of a child's lifelong reactions to stress.[2] I experienced a youth filled with trauma and an adulthood with ongoing traumas and tremendous stress. I really could have used that fortifying dosing of oxytocin!

Beginning as an infant, I screamed when my ears ruptured with sudden searing pain. I screamed when I couldn't hear words or songs and when others couldn't understand my words or songs. I screamed without success and then I fell into vast periods of solitary silence, retreating to the inner world. A world of different sounds.

This is one of my earliest childhood memories: A pale house. Wooden dining furniture, cream walls, brown sofa and tables. There was a great window looking into a square yard on my left, as I stood with my back to the kitchen doorway. My mother sat stiffly on the sofa, sewing. My father was bent before me, calm voice coaxing me to say it again. "I want a grape popsicle," I said. I was three years old.

I stamped my foot and spoke louder, thinking they couldn't hear me like I sometimes couldn't hear others' speech. "I want a grape popsicle!"

"What is she so upset about this time?" my mother said, sewing hands frozen with thread stretched quivering in the air, a quilt draped over her knees.

"I don't know. Say it one more time, Doren." My father was kneeling down watching my lips.

This time I screamed, "I want a grape popsicle!" I pointed to the kitchen behind me.

"I think she wants something from the kitchen," he said then, and walked into the kitchen. I followed.

Then began another set of questions with gestures, the fridge open, me pointing to the freezer. At last, the popsicle box coming out. I chose a purple one and my father ripped the package open. I put the popsicle in my mouth, went to the great window and sat looking out on the day.

The frozen treat cooled the fiery frustration in my belly while I listened to my parents' rising and falling murmur behind me. I did and didn't hear what they were saying. But the meaning was clear: They were talking about their troublesome girl.

Not long after this I had another unforgettable experience. It was an autumn ride in the car. I remember a euphoric sense of calm as I fixed my eyes up toward the tree canopy. Red, yellow, orange, and green leaves dancing to the silence of our passing. It was so beautiful! It was as if the frustration of my life had momentarily been given a stay, a breath with the trees. In the front seat, my parents were silent. They were calm also, finally knowing why their little girl was so terribly frustrated all the time. I couldn't hear.

Meanwhile, the doctors who had tested me at the clinic at the end of this tree-lined drive, explained that chronic hearing loss had resulted in my strange babbling language. Surgeries would begin in an effort to alter the problem. Most children grew out of it. I never would. But for that stretched out moment, nothing broke the beauty. Screams were patient.

I have a common childhood condition: Eustachian tube disfunction. The Eustachian tube is a tiny organ in the ear that mediates pressure and helps relieve the inner ear of fluids that accumulate with infection. My case was severe. I had frequent ear infections (perhaps caused by a struggling immune system and undiagnosed allergies to dairy and gluten), lasting into late adulthood. Before the age of twelve, I'd had eight surgeries under general anesthetic, to insert simulated tubes in my ear drums, but my body always quickly rejected the tubes.

This condition had a very interesting influence on my interpersonal and intra-personal skills. I could take minimal auditory cues, facial and body expressions, and perhaps otherworldly sensitivities, and combine them to understand people. My family had no idea that I couldn't hear for the first few years of my life because I was so good at this. Where I excelled in piecing together the incomplete into comprehension, they struggled to understand me, my pain, frustrations and indigo-child experiences. At the age of four, as a result of my second surgery, I began to speak, suddenly, in complete sentences.

Oddly, I was also naturally musical. I sang as a young child and throughout much of my life. I could hear my own voice resonating inside of my head, and I imagine I experienced it as a kind of self-soothing caress. I could hear music when I listened to people's voices—not the specific clear delineation of words—the rhythms, inflections and dynamics of expression.

I developed a heightened sense of empathy and additional senses which I would categorize as psychic. I posit that my difficulties with hearing the outer world, increased my sensitivities to hearing the spiritual world. I remember being immensely confused by the discrepancies between what a person said and what they emoted. As a very young child, I saw the lies of the world darken the truths of the soul, and I raged at those lies.

In addition to the lack of oxytocin, the frustration of pain and hearing problems, my biography included abandonment. By the time I was seven years old, my parents had married and divorced each other twice.

The first time they divorced, I was two. My father abandoned his law clerk job and his family. I don't remember much from this time period, but I know my mother was bitter and angry about my father's betrayal.

Once, my father suddenly showed up sporting a beard. He reached out to hold me and I responded with screaming and crying. I remember my mother shouting at him, and how he took a seat by the door smiling at me. I think it was her shouting that alerted me. This was my father! I jumped up and climbed onto his lap while they argued.

Two years later, after reuniting in marriage and relocating from Denver to California, my little sister was added to the family. My parents were doing their best. I remember that Jenna came home from the hospital with presents for her siblings. I loved my little baby doll in a pink flowered blanket. I remember folk songs around campfires and play dates with my friends. I gained my love of singing and walking, from being allowed to walk myself to kindergarten every morning.

When I was seven years old, my parents divorced a second time. We were all seated in the living room when they told us the news. They calmly explained how important it was for people to be happy, and that they weren't happy living together. This time, my mother would be moving into her own apartment. It seemed strange and sad to me, that my mother's happiness meant leaving her children. This time, I was left bitter and angry at my mother's betrayal.

From the age of seven to twelve, my parents traded their three children in complex and ever changing patterns. My brother and I were primarily in the care of my mother, and my little sister lived with our father. On weekends we three were together or traded between our parents. Both my father and mother moved often, which made me confused and scared, especially sleeping in new and different places.

This also necessitated midyear transfers to new schools and having to build new friendships. It was easier to be friends with my older brother. He had always been in my life. But Marc made me pass difficult dares and initiations in order to play with him and his friends. I became a hyperactive daredevil. With my chronic hearing problems, the school changes were difficult, and I often fought with others in school, got in trouble, and was misunderstood by my teachers.

I continued to be a difficult child. My mother, having had a tumultuous and painful relationship with her own critical mother, transferred those behaviors to me. We argued often, where I would scream and tantrum and she would respond with cruel words and impatient frustration. I felt unloved, misunderstood, and angry at her for applying herself to long hours working followed by a focus on numerous strange men who would become, for a brief time, my new father figures. In contrast, I enjoyed my father's frequent girlfriends, feeling the temporary affection of women who hadn't yet tired of me.

I remember my first cigarette at the age of twelve, stolen from my mother's cigarette purse. It was a rectangular, beige leather purse with a brass clasp, a perfect fit for her long thin cigarettes. After we'd had a bitter fight, she took a cigarette out of the purse, lit it and stomped out of the room. I snapped open the clasp, stole a cigarette, grabbed a pack of matches from a kitchen drawer and secreted myself to the side of the house where I took my first long inhales of smoky calm.

I didn't cough like movie renditions of a first cigarette. I inhaled the smoke, followed by a long indrawn breath—just like my mother—and held it in. In moments, I was slightly dizzy, calm, and my rage had completely subsided!

It was not long after this, that my mother packed my things up one day and delivered me to my father's door with the words: "You take her. I can't deal with her anymore!"

My mother's cigarettes were rarely close at hand, but my taste for the calm that cigarettes provided had been set. I now had to find new ways to acquire a cigarette and a chance to smoke. I frequented the neighborhood pool hall, begged cigarettes from its other patrons who taught me how to play pool. Smokers became my new friends, gladly trading a smoke for a conversation. Sometimes, I purchased a pack myself from the cigarette machine by the front door.

2. Takeda, Satoru, Yoshinori Kuwabara, and Masahiko Mizuno. "Concentrations and Origin of Oxytocin in Breast Milk." Endocrinologia Japonica Endocrinol Japon 33.6 (1986): 821-26. Web.

Sex, Cigarettes and Addiction

"Misunderstood, it pains me to cut you sharply and you shout. Misunderstood. it pains me to be the mirror that blinds you in the sun. I cry out silently, unheard, for it to stop, for you to heal from your gangrene, for you to see what I have only reflected. You think I am unaffected. But I am caught in the hands of your shining karma."

— *A Bright Sharp Tool*

My teen years were spent primarily under the strange and fairly negligent care of my father, who believed that children should be free to choose their own paths through life. I believed my mother didn't love me, and my father's love was expressed by long talks that he thought mediated complete freedom. At twelve years of age, I began to roam the streets of Berkeley and Oakland, dusk or dawn, it didn't matter. I'd socialize with people much older, sometimes with dangerous results.

For a time, I transferred much of my urge to scream into long walks and singing in the streets. I was wild and beautiful, unencumbered by the usual chains of parental supervision. I was lost in my inner world where the outer world of sound barely penetrated, yet I was extremely sensitive to the places and people I met as I roamed. I had not really developed strong boundaries. My mother was basically unavailable and my father did not believe in enforcing restrictions on my impulses.

Fact: The adolescent brain is in a highly developmental stage from the onset of puberty into the early 20s; subcortical limbic structures important for emotional processing, such as the hypothalamus, midbrain dopamine areas (those directly affected by nicotine), and the amygdala, are all in a huge growth phase. The maturation of these areas is very important for social and sexual behaviors triggered by pubertal hormones. In contrast, the frontal cortical areas of the adolescent brain, responsible for cognitive control over behavior, are undeveloped.[3] During this period of my life when I was most in need of parental support, I was left vulnerable and without cognitive controls.

When I was almost thirteen years old, I fell in love with a young man three and a half years older than me. Destiny called me to him, promising perfection and heartbreak. When I looked into his brown eyes I felt like I'd known him forever. When I stood next to him, my skin tingled and the world seemed brighter. Maybe it was the elusive work of pheromones, matching us for reproduction. Or the fact that love ignites oxytocin in the brain.

But it was a hopeless love. He already had a lover. He also had a younger sister the same age as me. Although he found me attractive and we socialized in the same circles, he had a sensibility that forbade him from taking advantage of someone so young.

I was devastated. However, even a year later, I was determinedly still in love. Almost fourteen, I decided to prove to him that I wan't too young to be sexually active. Everyone in my social group was sexually active. It was Berkeley in the '70s. If I could prove myself worthy of being his lover, I might have my fill of the love I craved.

I set my eyes on another young man in our social circle, and began to flirt with him. He was seven years older than me when we started dating. He was also somewhat disconcerted by my young age. And although he wasn't a virgin, he respected my virginity. For several months we had long make-out sessions, hugging and kissing. His college roommates were having sex with their same-age partners, but he was waiting for me. I felt a little guilty.

I pined for the man whose deep brown eyes touched my soul. I had gotten it into my head that if I wasn't a virgin, I might have a chance with the man I secretly wanted. I had used my boyfriend, but he wasn't going to take advantage of me. I'd have to press him to take my virginity. So I did, sweetly urging him to have sex with me, telling him I wanted to be a woman.

I was persuasive and he was twenty-one, in his hormonal prime. He began to consider it, but asked me to talk to my friends, my mother, to think about it further.

My first sexual encounter was imminent. But I took his words to heart, discussing sex with my sexually active friends of the same age. They all enjoyed sex and told me that if I liked kissing, then sex would be a delightful physical communion. Finally, I went to my mother's house to discuss it with her.

"Mom," I said as she sat at her dining room table smoking a cigarette, "I want to have sex with my boyfriend who is twenty-one. What do you think I should do? Should I have sex, or wait?"

I've never forgotten her reply. She took a puff on her cigarette, and tilting her chin up, she blew the smoke out in a long stream.

"You should go ahead, Doren," she said after a loud breath. "Older men are better lovers."

Now, I cringe when I think about it. I knew inside my heart that I was still too young. I'd gone to my mother hoping she'd stop me from this irrevocable decision. I was angry and in shock that she didn't seem to care if I had sex. Maybe she thought I was trying to shock her. I had always been stubborn, and by that time had often rebelled against her attempts to control me. Maybe she couldn't cope with the question, or she'd already written me off, thinking it wouldn't matter what she said. Either way, I figured, she'd given me her permission and I communicated that to my boyfriend.

A short while later, my boyfriend and I had sex in my father's house. He was kind and gentle, but the act itself felt hollow and strange. My first time having sex was painful and there weren't pleasurable sensations or euphoria. I thought it was because I loved a different man. I remember when we finished, how satisfied he appeared, and how badly I wanted a cigarette.

Fact: Cigarette smoking is known to be highly addictive because of its efficient delivery of nicotine to the brain and the brain's resulting dependency on tobacco-induced dopamine production. Nicotine activates the circuitry that regulates feelings of pleasure and reward. It has both stimulating and sedative effects. Within 10 seconds of inhalation, nicotine activates the dopamine receptors in the brain, providing soothing feelings of pleasure. The use of cigarettes also creates a complex dependency, especially in developing brains, as it lowers the brain's own capacity for maintaining required dopamine levels.[4]

Scientists are not certain which of the approximately 4000 chemicals present in cigarettes has this additional psychoactive effect. What they do know is that tobacco smoke also decreases monoamineoxidase (MAO), an enzyme responsible for breaking down dopamine. The tobacco assisted decrease in MAO results in the presence of higher dopamine levels. However, nicotine is eliminated by the body rapidly. This increases the desire for repeated smoking to replicate short-lived feelings of pleasure, calm and increased attention. The receptors in the brain undergo complex adaptive changes including upregulation (an increase of a cellular response to a stimulus) and desensitization. Over time, these changes contribute to a stronger need for nicotine stimulation to achieve the rewards of smoking.[5]

Despite my carnal discrepancy, I wanted sex to be an expression of love. I look back now, and realize I was desperate to feel love igniting my heart, my body and brain. I knew my decision had been wrong for me, and I was disappointed with myself. How immature I was despite all my intuitive strengths. Sex changed everything and nothing. I had been initiated into the sacred circle of womanhood, but at a price. I was still hungry for love.

By the age of fourteen, I'd learned that I was basically on my own, realizing my screams would not be met with ameliorating love and support from my mother. I'd learned that I couldn't be with the man I loved, and that loving the one you're with is a hollow substitute; by the age of fourteen I filled these hollow spaces with cigarettes, and the chemical production of dopamine that cigarettes provided. Yes, cigarettes made me feel happy. They helped me deal with familial rejection, manage emotional disappointments, and less than a year later, cigarettes would also help me survive rape. My fourteenth year was a slow and steady destruction of my wild beauty, where cigarettes became a self-sabotaging coping strategy for my troubled existence. Cigarettes were available to me, and they were effective.

3. Goriounova, Natalia A., and Huibert D. Mansvelder. "Short- and Long-Term Consequences of Nicotine Exposure during Adolescence for Prefrontal Cortex Neuronal Network Function." Cold Spring Harbor Perspectives in Medicine. U.S. National Library of Medicine, 01 Dec. 2012. Web. 3 May 2016.

4. "Psychology Today." Nicotine. N.p., n.d. Web. 16 June 2016. Source: National Institute on Drug Abuse. <https://www.psychologytoday.com/conditions/nico-tine>

5. ECigaretteUSA. "Nicotine in the Brain." YouTube. YouTube, 2009. Web. 4 May 2016. <https://www.youtube.com/watch?v=yoOLVM1U5L8>

Young Feminist Cigarette Fortress

"Oh humans! I tire so easily from the patterns of your lies. Cracked and dirty tombs choking off the power of my speech. Preventing me from leaping ahead into the beautiful moments with you."

— *A Volcano Once Dormant*

For much of my life, I spent inordinate amounts of energy arguing with the hypocrisies I observed in people and societies. It drove me to intense bouts of frustration when people would say one thing and do something in contradiction to their words. Or pretend to stand for noble truths, then be afraid to act upon that knowledge.

My keen sense for justice and my quick mind were impatient with the complex solutions our societal problems require. People have an instinctual need to reproduce and care for their young, yet we do things that harm future generations. This contradiction resulted in painful and overwhelming cognitive dissonance.

Out of the chaos I cried for simple solutions. Why can't we just be honest with each other? Why can't we feed the hungry everywhere? Why don't we care for our global resources? Why can't I scream when I'm angry?

My family and friends experienced the brunt of this in frequent argument and in my tendency to shout as I became frustrated. My teachers experienced it also. Having me as a student included dealing with my creative and logical rebellions.

I remember once, during a period of hearing loss, reading my entire fourth grade history book instead of trying to listen to the teacher's lessons. One day, having completed reading the text, I raised my hand and asked my teacher why there were so few women described in our American history book.

She replied that history books record the lives and works of important people who have done important things. She explained that American history focuses on the lives and actions of famous men because men have been at the forefront of important events.

I argued that there had to be women who participated in every important event.

"Women are everywhere, as mothers, sisters and daughters," I told her. "They had to be at those important events. Who were they? Why aren't they mentioned in the stories?"

"Women didn't do that many important things," she replied. "They weren't allowed to participate in historical events. That's why the women's suffrage movement was important."

I understood this. I'd read the book. But there was still a flaw in her position and I tried to explain it to her. My argument went something like this:

"Women have always been a part of history. Every man has been brought into the world and raised by a mother. There had to be brave and powerful women at all those important events in history. Where men may have fought battles, I know women were caring for the sons that fought and died. Where men argued about founding philosophies, I know that women were voicing their thoughts, even if it was just at home. Women were essential to westward expansion. Women won their right to vote, and achieved equal recognition according to the law. So why doesn't our history book give them equal exposure now? There are only two sections in the whole book, that talk about women."

I remember the intensity of my anger, and how my teacher didn't acknowledge the point I was trying to make. My words had also angered her, but my inquiries left her without a better response than, "you should be paying attention to the lesson instead of reading the book."

But I had read the book! I'd learned about all the original Americans that had been killed and relocated by colonists. How people kill over ideological and religious differences. That declarations of independence were only created for certain people: white men and property owners. I'd learned about how the beautiful air and lands of America were overwhelmed by industrial pollution. I'd learned that justice required brave voices and a willingness to struggle.

I didn't know it then, but I was a young feminist. My brave voice had been a distraction in the machinery of our school day, but it was impossible to halt these impulses. I often raged at my existence as a female and the vulnerability that gave me. I sometimes thought it would be better to have been born a man, to have superior strength, inferred power, freedom. I imagined that as a man it would be safe to travel and I could do whatever I wanted to do with my life.

Cigarettes hardened me. When I smoked I felt tough, stronger, more capable. I knew that my sensitivities made me vulnerable. My empathy connected me to the world's pain. It was overwhelming and devastating when I realized how powerless I was to change the world, much less others. Why did I have this capacity if I could do nothing? However, standing on the street with my cigarette, made me a fortress that could withstand the terrors of the world.

Ritual Incense, Temple Market Sacrifice

"If I could scream at any necessary time, or go hunting for days, I would smoke much less, perhaps not at all."

— *A Cigarette At The Edge Of The World*

As a very young child, I had discovered a love of Christ. For a few years, when my parents were still together, we attended a Presbyterian church. I enjoyed the gatherings, dressing up, the joyous spiritual music and playing with friends on the church's front lawn.

Around the corner from our house, lived a very old woman. She used to invite the neighborhood children over to listen to bible verses. I went there often, to sit in her pretty house and listen to the melodic mumble of her voice. After the requisite verse, she would proffer a crystal dish filled with candy. I associated those verses with the sweetness of candy, with the elegant soft-voiced beauty of that old woman and her home. Her faith was merry and resonated love. And I had a sweet tooth.

When my parents divorced, for the second time, we no longer attended church. My mother had decided to become a Buddhist. My father was an intellectual, pursuing magic, Gnostic Christian philosophies and spiritual study through books and personal rituals.

Despite my parents' differing paths, my love of Christ continued to grow. The basic tenet of Christianity made sense to me. There was a creator who'd given us a compassionate teacher to lead us through the door of eternal life. But the other churches I encountered when occasionally attending with friends' families, were rife with judgment and hellfire. This did not align with the love, compassion and forgiveness Christ taught.

My wandering youth, introduced me to pagan social groups in Berkeley, benign Wiccan and Goddess worshipers. I was intrigued by their reverence of feminine power, love of nature, by their beautiful rituals and gatherings. This was the first place I felt I could be honest about my personal psychic experiences. Yet these circles also left me unsatisfied. Many of these individuals were adamantly against my spiritual kin who followed Christ.

These conflicting truths left me unsettled and bitter. Patriarchal religions confused and angered me, and the Christian institution had elements I couldn't reconcile: stringent rules regarding expressions of love and the nature of spiritual reality, hypocritical tendencies to judgment, brutal histories of conquering various peoples, unequal relationships among men and women, and religious propaganda. At the same time, I was disappointed and surprised by the closed minds of my pagan friends. They expressed rampant disdain for people who were moved by the Christ impulse, which included me.

Over time, I created my own amalgamated philosophy, one which aligned with the instincts of my heart. No human owns the patent to revelation. It seemed only logical to me, that all spiritual traditions held some part of truth. The wise ones that came before me, and from whom we gain philosophical knowledge and religious traditions, discovered some truths during their lives. Just like them, I would discover truth for myself.

I couldn't understand how religions divided people. I could see the divine in everyone. Why didn't other people also recognize the shared divine nature of all people, regardless of religious upbringing or attraction?

I always felt like a stranger wherever I wandered. But I tried to remain true to my self. I prayed for street people that I met as I roamed. I talked to God aloud, and sang Christian songs. Christmas and Easter filled me with awe as I contemplated Christ, the stories of His birth and sacrifice. I also participated in ceremonious activities with pagan friends. I played the role of maiden in a Goddess play at a Unitarian church. I burned sage and chanted on full moon hikes in the Berkeley hills; and celebrated people in all their complex and varied beauty, as children of heaven and earth.

I tried to explain my thinking to people. When I was among pagans, I felt the powerful heartbeat of the Mother in the wonders of nature. But I wanted them to know the love of Christ. I wanted them to understand that what Christ taught had nothing to do with the crimes perpetrated by Christian institutions throughout history. It hurt when I would hear these people criticize Christians or the Christian church. Instead of being an empowering experience, I felt that my love of Christ had to be constrained.

When I was among my Christian brethren, I wanted them to acknowledge the creative forces of nature and the divine Mother. These people had a vast respect for the environment, were actively protecting nature and promoting wellness based on the awesome capacities of creation. There were women among the Goddess worshipers that played a significant role in guiding me during my teen years. They mentored my love of natural foods and alternative health care. I knew instinctively that we are entrusted to love and steward the earth and all its creatures. I wanted Christians to see and act on these universal truths.

My attempts to reconcile for others what made the most sense to me, often led to conflict. Hefty debates with people who had more biblical knowledge, maturity or social and historical savvy than I, led to feelings of inadequacy and frustration. My shouts were considered incongruous to the peaceful exclusion practiced by the religious and spiritual groups I encountered.

Yet l was cognizant that l didn't accept how people chose to align them-selves. l was equally capable of conflicting thoughts, emotions and deeds. My own error laden decisions and tendencies filled me with self recrimination. My attempts to speak of justice were often rife with failure. l was demoralized by the human tendency to corruption, by criticism, division and misunderstanding, and by my own inner voice expecting so much more from myself. l felt ashamed by my hypocritical outbursts, and was simultaneously hurt by the reactions of people l respected.

One day, l encountered a group of Quakers. The Quakers were Christian. They were also devoted advocates for social justice. l attended a few informal meetings where friends would sit in silent contemplation and prayer for an hour. The silence was followed by words and songs, from anyone in the group who felt moved to share. l thought for a brief time, that l'd come home.

Once l rose from the hour of silence and proceeded to sing. My improvised song, filled with inspired innocence, was about the elements of fire, water, air, earth and spirit. lt spoke of how we are all connected, both nature and human, all endowed with spirit and consciousness. The facilitator of the meeting admonished me with his eyes. lt was a clear message that l wasn't on point, l didn't have a right to speak my truth openly in this circle either.

All of these experiences kept me searching for a spiritual home, and walking away unsatisfied. Eventually, l learned to speak the language of the people whose circles l had temporarily joined, to discriminate between what was accepted within the confines of their philosophies and what was not. l learned to silence my words of kinship beyond differences. l learned to hold secret my visions and intuitions. Where my spiritual or religious inclinations might have satisfied my need for love, l found a further sense of alienation.

l searched and l waited. l was waiting for a place that could hold all of my truth. l was waiting for the day my screams about intolerance and division might one day be valued and accepted, without requiring that l change the nature of my tune. Waiting until l knew how to be a peacemaker myself, until l had the right words to convince and motivate others to see what l saw.

Cigarettes helped me wait. They were my ritual incense, my temple market sacrifice. Cigarettes were my companion in silence.

lt would be many years before l understood: The world is my church, and life my worship.

Lucid Dreaming and Insanity

"But you knot the soon to come as if it were a wild horse to be broken, not a gift to be savored. And I sit unwinding a moment."

— *Alas, I Ramble*

For much of my youth, I had been hearing voices: some of which could easily be cast as imaginary friends; however, I determined that some were spirit guides or angels, while others I interpreted as ghosts or ancestors. I took these experiences and my interpretations in stride. This was my normal. My logical mind sought adequate theories for my reality.

Yet I often questioned the nature of these voices. At times I tried to deny or halt these and other psychic experiences that made my life confusing and difficult. I wanted to fit into some societal normal, to belong. This vacillating struggle to either integrate or deny continued until I was much older.

In my youth, I encountered many significant premonitory moments in dreams and awake. This occurred in childhood, as a teenager, and continues to this day. I was keenly aware of the significance of these events because my premonitions so often came true. The ability to know who is calling on the phone, or to have prescient indications of events in the lives of the self and loved ones, is fairly common. Explaining these things in terms of the the brain's capacity to interpret vast amounts of sensory data and decipher future probabilities, seems appropriate. For a long time this explanation satisfied my logical mind. That is, until sensory data was completely unavailable and premonition still occurred.

In addition to my experiences of hearing non-physical entities and my improbable yet fairly frequent premonitions, I am a lucid dreamer. Lucid dreaming is a dream state of heightened awareness in which it is common for people to consciously influence the nature of their dreams.

I had always had powerful and intense experiences in my dream life, to include clear messages and lessons while sleeping, premonitions, and lucidity. I was a frequent sleepwalker in my youth. I have been a victim to what is described as night terrors. But when I was fourteen years old, I began going to sleep while awake, never losing consciousness even as I shifted from waking to dreaming.

For almost two years, I regularly went to sleep awake (as often as four or five nights a week) and experienced highly lucid states while dreaming. I remember distinctly, the first time this occurred. I felt as if I had fallen through my belly and then found myself sitting before a large wooden table in a vast library. In front of me lay a book with glowing words. A door opened to my right, and a man in robes and head cloth with a long white beard, said: "You are not ready yet."

I returned immediately, as if tugged back into my body by a tether attached to my belly.

I went to sleep again and again that night, each time, experiencing no loss of consciousness. I had distinct sensations of dropping through my belly, then would find myself floating above my body. I could see my room clearly and my body prone below. The transition without loss of consciousness filled me with an inextricable fear that my body was vulnerable without me in it. I woke terrified and crying out. Then I closed my eyes and repeated the experience, until finally, after countless times, I fell asleep with the gift of total exhaustion.

If it had been a one night occurrence I probably would have dismissed it as a strange and terrifying nightmare. But the falling asleep awake happened over and over again for almost two years! Thus began an intense period of study, where I read all I could find about astral travel, and recorded experiments as I tried to develop some control over my experiences. I became lucid at different stages of sleep. Sometimes I would go to sleep awake and I'd try to maintain my awareness for as long as possible without returning to my body. I'd awaken in my body again, or eventually drift into dreams or the darkness of deep sleep. Sometimes, I'd wake within a dream, and practice various controls, traveling to specific places and visiting people I knew in their dreams. Later, my friends would be surprised by how I could tell them what they had dreamed. Eventually, I began to find myself in the lucid state early morning hours; I'd fly through the world and see what people were doing around me, what they were wearing, which room of the house they were in, what my neighbors were having for breakfast, etc, and then I'd quickly wake in my body, and I'd run to see whether my dream visions were true. They were! These experiences established for me, without a doubt, an understanding that we are infinitely more complex than mere physical matter.

Unfortunately, during much of my youth—particularly during this time—I also came in contact with entities that I would describe as evil. I was as much traumatized by being abandoned and raped as I was by struggling to understand the nature of my astral travel and some of the things I encountered during that time. I became even more religious, seeking the protection and guidance of God and angels to help me through these difficult ordeals. The frequency of my lucid dreaming shifted as I grew, though it has never altogether disappeared.

I sometimes wonder if cigarettes helped stop this difficult happening of lucid dreaming. I know they helped me ameliorate my fear and cope through crisis. I remember distinct moments where I would wake from an encounter with something terrifying, and immediately smoke a cigarette in the dark comfort of the physical world.

Some people would suggest that the symptomatic experiences I've described above, were the result of what psychologists term schizophrenia. However, even though I've shared my history fully and honestly with doctors and therapists, they've never placed me in this category. In the light of what I know, I question the purely biological explanations of schizophrenic mania. I'm sure there is a chemical element that is somewhat balanced by psychotropic medicines and can be made more extreme by the use of other drugs. But I believe that our society doesn't quite know how to adequately help people who experience visions, voices and encounters with non-physical entities.

I have, however, been given a diagnosis of bipolar 1 disorder. I don't altogether argue with this description, but I believe that my life expressions and circumstances are far more complex than a set of relatively random criteria set in a psychological manual—feigned apologies to the DSM IV and V. Psychologists are at the work of quantifying spirit and consciousness in materialistic terms, and as my super-sensible experiences attest, this is an incomplete manner of explanation.

A person affected by bipolar 1 disorder has had at least one manic episode in life. A manic episode is a period of abnormally elevated mood and high energy, accompanied by abnormal behavior that disrupts life.[6] During the period of my lucid entry into sleep at the age of fourteen, I chose to leave behind the friends I'd made in Berkeley, many of whom were experimenting with dangerous drugs. I lived for a brief time on a ranch in Siskiyou county—this was perhaps my first manic decision—which my parents' supported as an attempt to help me change my lifestyle. In addition to manic behavior, people with bipolar 1 disorder are also described as suffering from episodes of depression. I have certainly struggled with periods of paralyzing hopelessness and feelings of depression. While these feelings are often related to personal events in my life, they all stem from feelings about injustice and suffering throughout the world, and my inability to alter these realities.

I question the diagnosis, causes and remedies for my struggles. While there are familial histories of mania and depression, I wonder if my super-sensible abilities, life challenges, prolonged periods of stress and the traumas I've experienced haven't been the greater cause of sadness and instability. I have come to believe that my suffering, that all suffering, serves to help us learn compassion and love. I've applied my considerable intelligence and energy to understanding and supporting myself through the conditions and experiences of my biography. And I believe, that if the world was a place of greater harmony and justice, if my parents had been more stable and supportive, I would not have experienced such intense feelings of anger and hopelessness. Yet, I am grateful for my biography and all that it has taught me.

I'm sure that both the causes and the mediating remedies for what is perceived as mental illness are numerous and complex. However, I would not relegate my wellness to the pharmacological experimentations of recent medicine to manage life, just as I do not depend on prayer alone. Toxins in the environment are also surely culprits that have affected my wellness and I know that frequent bouts of anxiety, as well as several health problems, disappeared when I completely stopped ingesting gluten—sudden anxiety is my first symptom with accidental gluten poisoning. I also know PTSD (Post Traumatic Stress Disorder) episodes have become much less frequent since I removed myself from stressful and unsupportive environments, and from toxic people. My recovery from PTSD episodes has become much more rapid since I've learned to manage them with cognitive behavioral methods. I am a fan of organic food, alternative remedies and lifestyle changes as the first and frontline defense against all calamities, in addition to spiritual and community support.

My relationship to smoking and my choice to continue smoking as a strategic tool, is directly related to what I would call "the spiritual burdens or opportunities of my biography," and it is also supported by neuroscience. I am intrigued by both the developmental and the palliative correlations discovered between cigarette smoking and mental illness/duress. Studies show that there is a high rate of cigarette use among people with mental illness, who most likely use nicotine to manage or mask symptoms. However, there are also studies that demonstrate people with depression, schizophrenia and PTSD can quit without impairing their mental health recovery.[7] There is certainly a concurrent and mutually influential relationship between environment and biology, and successful cessation of smoking for people with mental illness is maximized by therapeutic treatment and supports.

Nevertheless, when I apply honest reflection to my experiences I cannot accept a purely psychopathological paradigm. It doesn't make logical sense! The life of matter is not separated from the life of spirit, regardless of current trends to collapse consciousness into a 3.5 pound spherical blob of "gray" matter. Spirit exists and is intricately woven through the body and consciousness of the individual biography and the shared global biography. What I know (but others might categorize as my belief) is that the biography is perfectly designed to educate us and help us evolve as spiritual beings.

As a human organism, we debate the mythology of various religions, the validity of spiritual or scientific world views, and the nature or cause of the experience of consciousness. We have rich traditions, teachings, and demonstrations of how consciousness defies the conceived limits of matter. We attempt to catalogue the inner world through electrical impulses with growing (and fascinating) explorations into brain chemistry. Quantum Physics entertains us with new theoretical discussions on the nature of energy and matter. Science is a popular means of exploring consciousness, but so are spiritual teachings.

So, am I crazy or on a narrow path of enlightenment? I would suggest that I am both—as the terms are useful and not mutually exclusive.

6. *"Bipolar l Disorder Symptoms, Treatments, Causes, and More." WebMD. Web-MD, n.d. Web. 5 May 2016. <http://www.webmd.com/bipolar-disorder/guide/bi-polar-1-disorder>*

7. *Weir, K. "Smoking and Mental lllness." Monitor on Psychology, 23 June 2013. Web. 5 May 2016. <http://www.apa.org/monitor/2013/06/smoking.aspx>*

Rape and a Spider's Web of PTSD

"Just cold numb nothingness, nothing but a cigarette. So good in the rain. To remind you that you are alive, you are breathing. And the rain falls for you, for all the tears you can cry, or can't cry, trying to cry away those memories. Corrupted interrupted amygdala dendrites. And how they painted the rest of your life in tile and glass cages where no one can hear you, even if you do scream."

—In Tile and Glass Cages

Cigarettes provided me with helpful dopamine production and a dangerously addictive habit. I've had doctors literally tell me not to quit smoking, stating that smoking helps me cope with PTSD and bipolar 1 disorder. I could have taken this advise as a license to smoke. But what I've done, what I'm doing right now, is taking it as an opportunity to explore the intricacies of compassion and nonjudgmental, or "redemptive" thinking.

The biography is an amazing thing. Even our life challenges and wounds can be harnessed into gifts, love and learning. We use the power of consciousness and the heart of compassion to redeem ourselves and others. My gift of heightened empathy skills and capacity to read people beyond the words they use, found expression as a teacher of children with special needs. My experiences with psychic phenomena, which can only be fully understood as of a spiritual nature, required that I be highly reflective about life events and the nature of consciousness. My journey has been one of learning to love myself despite my challenges and flaws, attempting to apply that same kind of love to the families and students in my care, as well as to the people that have harmed me. It has helped me to view a world filled with injustice as a school for developing love.

Fact: I've been raped numerous times, and while that's horrifying, cigarettes have helped me through the traumatic experience. To this day, talking about my stories of rape feels a bit dangerous. The night before last, I had a terrible nightmare where I was bound and tortured by a man with a knife. Having once been threatened with a knife, and once abducted and bound for a night of multiple rapes, I am not surprised by this nightmare. This morning, I woke with intense anxiety. I questioned what I'm doing, what I'm sharing in this narrative, and recognize that the writing is a trigger for my PTSD.

Post Traumatic Stress Disorder is diagnosed after a person experiences symptoms following a traumatic event. Symptoms may not appear until several months or even years later. There are three main types of symptoms: Re-experiencing trauma through recollections, flashbacks and nightmares. Emotional numbness and avoidance of places, people and activities that are reminders of the trauma. Difficulty sleeping or concentrating and feelings of anxiety, irritability or anger. When a person is experiencing an episode of PTSD it can feel like the trauma is happening all over again. This disorder also includes persistent negative beliefs, persistent fear or shame, feelings of detachment, reckless or self-destructive behavior, and hyper-vigilance, to name a few.[8]

PTSD triggers the fight-or-flight reflex of the amygdala, a region of the brain that helps us process emotions and fear responses.[9] Unfortunately, the amygdala in PTSD sufferers is hyperactive, so that fear and stress responses can be heightened even when confronted with stimuli not associated with the original trauma.[10]

I find myself asking, "Should I stop right now? Abandon the addition of this narrative in my book of poetry and photographs?"

"No," I tell myself. "I'd rather push through to the other side." I light a cigarette and continue.

PTSD. It's like a spider's web. You're always trapped in it. Sometimes you can't see the lines constricting your life, you're just swinging along. Sometimes you can see the spider coming for you, and you're stuck there knowing it's coming. But everyone else likes to tell you that you're not stuck. Or they like to think you're wrong about the spider. And then, there are the times, it just takes a bite when you aren't even looking. You know, like those invisible spider bites you get just taking a walk on a beautiful spring morning. Except, it's not some benign itch that will disappear in a day. PTSD is here, forever. And that little bite, that wee little thing, it's deadly. Suddenly you feel its necrosis creeping under your skin and peeling it off. The pain is... unbearable, and you have to do something, anything, to try and stop it. Except you've been here before and you know: Nothing stops the torment. Maybe, time...if you survive.

So you get totally into survival mode. And that is different for different people. That's why it's so hard to understand PTSD when you aren't in its web. Some people survive with a gun, and that gun gets strapped on, or tucked in, or laid nearby. Before, they needed it, and now, they feel they might. Whereas some people survive with a drug, and that drug gets to wrapping them up in a little cocoon, not safe, not painless, just...numb. And some people survive with a hyper awareness of everything and everyone, and that means no sleep, because sleep is dangerous. It's in sleep that they've been traumatized. As for me? Well, I pray and I cry, and I wrap myself in a dark room, if I can. I smoke a cigarette to stay alert, to calm my brain, to cloak myself in the smoke of "I can take anything just a little bit longer."

Cigarette packs mark my timeline of surviving rape. The nightmare is surreal, different men and rapes writhing together like a nest of snakes in my memory. Before the age of fifteen, I was raped by several men over thirty—the oldest of which was nearly fifty years old. I can recall three specific men. And three specific rapes. Two were me, just frozen and waiting for it to be over, blaming myself for landing in the situation. The third was brutal. I fought and lost as he pounded above me, holding me down with his strong arms and shouting expletives. I remember thinking, "This man swears a lot."

When I was eighteen, I went on a date. The man abducted me to his house, tied me up and raped me several times throughout the night. Just when I thought it was over, he dragged me into a bathroom, beat me against the tile walls of the shower and I blacked out. Either I fainted and blacked out, or I disconnected from my body and disappeared to a safer place to survive the ordeal. I remember waking up in his car as he drove me home to where I was living with my mother for a short time. I told no one, but my mother and I proceeded to fight intensely and I moved out within a couple of months.

Shortly after the move, I began dating a man and watched that relationship disintegrate into domestic abuse as he became addicted to methamphetamines. I had not recovered from the brutal rape, and I was in shock and felt paralyzed by this new violence. He often choked me into unconsciousness and I would wake up to him raping me. When I finally found the courage to leave this man, he continued to harass and attack me.

I had no place to go, so I remained living in the same small town where he also lived. I got married, thinking that he would leave me alone if I was married. He didn't. When I was six months pregnant, he tried to run me over with a car. I was pulled to safety just in time. He was arrested. The day before Thanksgiving, I received a call that he'd been released from jail. I was eight months pregnant and terrified. Thankfully, he never attacked me again.

However, the damage was done. All of these violations were like napalm to my mind, heart and body.

So, do you feel it? The screaming? How it reaches for a cigarette? How the smoke eases the pain for a moment?

According to RAINN (Rape, Abuse & Incest National Network), 44% of sexual assault victims are under the age of 18 and 80% are under the age of 30. Each year in America, there are about 293,000 victims of sexual assault. 68% of sexual assaults are not reported to the police. 98% of rapists will never spend a day in jail or prison.[11]

None of my attackers, except for my boyfriend who tried to kill me with his car, have ever been prosecuted. I wish sometimes, that I could find them and hold them accountable for the damage they caused. This would be very difficult so many years since the assaults, and ultimately for me, it would not be a healthy focus of my energy. Certainly, I've experienced anger and rage at moments in my life since these atrocities were caused upon my person. I support women who confront rapists and bring them to justice. Even more importantly, we all must hold a no tolerance attitude and use the legal system and other methods to create effective deterrents to rape.

However, the predominant feeling I hold for the men who raped me, is compassion. I have chosen to recreate these experiences through love and redemptive thinking. Just as I have to live with the trauma, they have to live with their demons. Their actions were symptoms of a great evil, human wounds expressed through freedom. We are free to do wrong, and free to do right. Life is the school where we learn the consequences and rewards of our freedom.

I will not lie: Bathrooms are generally awful places for me. Stepping into a tiled shower stall is never easy, and sometimes, it's downright terrible. Taking a shower becomes an ordeal I work myself up to, survive, and then hope it doesn't have a lasting triggering effect of a PTSD episode. Often, I smoke before getting in the shower, the black calm forming a fortress against the memories.

The act of forgiveness is not always total forgetting. It is a conscientious decision. Forgiveness must be exercised and practiced. When thoughts of condemnation and feelings of rage or vengeance arise, we can transform them into understanding. The more we practice forgiveness and constructive responses to suffering, the stronger our moral body grows.

Often, the greater challenge is learning to treat our own mistakes with compassion and kindness. One of my favorite teachers, Don Miguel Ruiz, in his book, *The Four Agreements*, suggests that we acknowledge errors only one time.[12] Once our awareness lights upon a mistake, we do not need to relive and review that mistake again and again. Such thinking is a way of living in the past. We can agree instead, to focus our thinking on the present. This is what it means to do our best.

I've had powerful dreams where I meet these men and tell them I forgive them. Once, I dreamed of my boyfriend, the one who tried to kill me. After I had told him I forgive him, he told me he was trying to forgive himself. We were in a field of wild flowers under a beautiful afternoon sun. He picked me up gently in his strong arms, cradling me like a baby and walking through the tall grasses while I gazed at soft white clouds floating in the sky. Not all dreams are nightmares, and not all of my life is spent stuck in the spider's web.

I want rapists to be stopped, even incarcerated. I want rapists to contemplate their crimes in the light of ending such actions and reinventing themselves into better people. This is the best outcome I can imagine.

It is my spiritual beliefs which have helped me work to transform these dark seeds into flowers. My own shame at screaming in rage, or wishing violent and swift change in the world, is a kind of recognition of the potential for evil, even in myself. My beliefs in an afterlife and the nature of spiritual justice are distinct vessels for compassion and forgiveness. It is the cigarette that bolsters me through this transformation.

I believe we do experience an "eye for an eye," in the realm of spirit. When we die, that justice is carried out before our eyes. There, in a kaleidoscopic flash, we experience all we have done, or thought, through the perspective of those we've done it to. Thus, the men who harmed me and tormented my life with trauma, will or have already experienced what they did, as if it was done to them.

Even though I think we must end the societal structures that allow such evils to persist, I cannot wish anything worse on the men who harmed me. Not only will they experience my pain, but they will know they were the cause, and will be confronted with forgiving or condemning themselves. My inner work to forgive is something I hope they can experience. They too, were victims of societal error, an agreement to ignore or cope in silence with the atrocities we commit on each other.

As a society, we must create sure and safe spaces for all.

8. "Symptoms of PTSD." Anxiety and Depression Association of America. N.p., Apr. 2016. Web. 6 May 2016. < http://www.adaa.org/understanding-anxiety/post-traumatic-stress-disorder-ptsd/symptoms>

9. Smith, M., MD, R. Lawrence, and J. Segal, Ph.D. "PTSD: Symptoms, Self-Help, and Treatment." HelpGuide.org. N.p., May 2016. Web. 6 May 2016. < http://www.helpguide.org/articles/ptsd-trauma/post-traumatic-stress-disorder.htm>

10. Viatcheslav, W., Ph.D. "How Does Post-Traumatic Stress Disorder Change the Brain?" Brain Blogger How Does PostTraumatic Stress Disorder Change the Brain Comments. N.p., 1 Jan. 2015. Web. 6 May 2016. <http://brainblogger.com/2015/01/24/how-does-post-traumatic-stress-disorder-change-the-brain/>

11. "Statistics." RAINN |. N.p., n.d. Web. 6 May 2016. Rape, Abuse & Incest National Network. <https://www.rainn.org/statistics>

12. Ruiz, Miguel. The Four Agreements: A Practical Guide to Personal Freedom. San Rafael, CA: Amber-Allen Pub., 1997. Print. The Fourth Agreement: Do Your Best.

Epidemic of Silence

"Not just any moment. The one when you feel heaven fall out from under your wings. Sharp aloneness permeates your being. Every conversation, high tech coliseum—pause that white noise thought."

— A Pause on the Avalanche of Life

I believe that cigarettes are part of the bread and circus show designed to keep us from rising up out of insanity to claim a healthier and more just world. I smoke for the feelings of pleasure that smoking stimulates, to mask my pain and frustration, to distract from that which overwhelms me. The cigarette exists so that I remain quiet and complacent. The cigarette assures that I'll have the ongoing distractions of addiction, societal disdain and illness.

Moments of laughter are good medicine. I know that everyone suffers, and everyone tries to find joy. From the runner addicted to endorphins and the avid moviegoer, to the busy hobbyist or plethora of connoisseurs, we all engage ourselves in distractions. We need joy as much as we need water and air. For me, I love to be playful, throw a Frisbee, play board games, dance and diversify my social circles—both online and in the physical world.

I often wish I was not so sensitive and discontent, that I could submerse myself in joyous pursuits without rising for air with my screams. But sometimes, a chill thought seeps into laughter's warm conviction--even while watching my favorite Ellen DeGeneres clips. Odd moments or words will trigger impatience, sadness and pain. I find myself remembering how much injustice and corruption in our world still needs remedying. Even if I'm talking with someone about a hot topic during a party, I can observe my agitation as it rises, sometimes overflowing the floodgates I've so carefully placed upon myself.

It is in moments like these where I am met face to face with my own hypocrisy. I want to scream at the inadequacy of our societies, at my own inadequacy to eliminate injustice, poverty, hunger and pain. But joyous moments are not the place for these screams, not while the cake is being brought out, and certainly not mid-song. And so, I smoke. Where others may eat, drink, or others lose themselves in the many distractions that make life bearable and worthy, the cigarette I crave is a part of the circus I decry.

My last Christmas celebration with my father was one such occasion. After a delightful morning of baking gluten free scones and quiche, which we ate while opening presents, I lost my temper. My father was pleased to receive many gifts related to his favorite football team. He was looking forward to wearing his new jersey and drinking from his logo mug while watching the coming game. I began to share my frustration about football, how dangerous it is to the health of the young men we cast into the coliseum, how it is representative of big industry and unequal pay.

"Teachers' jobs", I said, "are highly stressful, practically 24/7, and we are 'on stage' for six hours a day without the benefit of assistants, catering and massage. Even champion teachers will never receive the salaries they deserve, and some of our worst students will become rich in the big industry of sports."

As I spoke, my voice rose and my monologues increased in length and frustration. My father was hurt by my rant, which had sliced into his joyous Christmas surprises. He accused me of "not understanding the perfection of creation," and of "being hypocritical," which made me even more angry. I stomped away, my final words flying loudly across the decorated Christmas tree, the piled collections of happy gifts and the discards of colorful wrapping paper. "I'm going for a smoke!"

I've learned that my agitation can come at the wrong time, in the middle of celebrations. I've learned to leave the party to take a walk and puff on a cigarette, or leave the conversation to gyrate wildly in dance. I know if I don't walk away, I'll start to scream whether metaphorically or literally. And I've learned that people aren't ready for my screams to tear through the shared spaces. Fact: Smoking replaces my need to scream.

Here is the cognitive dissonance. When I step away to smoke, I submit. I submit to patience for others and peace where I would wage global revolution. But even this makes me want to scream. For I am a revolutionary at war with my own peaceful philosophies. If perhaps, my screams for truth and justice were accepted by the people around me, I would have no need to smoke. Perhaps my screams are an atrocity committed upon the celebration of life. Perhaps what I need most is not in the screaming or the cigarette at all.

Many people have suffered far greater atrocities and trauma than I (war, famine, etc.), but they do not smoke or rely on chemical restraints. Instead, they've found healthier ways to cope, heal and joyously greet life. There are social and political activists who are awake and share my discontent with inequality and injustice. They've determined that right action should be dignified and nonviolent. They wage peace and patient community change. These people are my hope, and yet I still smoke.

Every one of us has our own perfect timing for growth. It's so much easier to contain the little problems of our own lives, then to feel the huge problems of the whole world, or even the problems of those we love. And sometimes, the singular problems of our own lives are enough to keep us fully challenged. Yet I'm acutely cognizant that a populace mired down by the needs of simple survival, benefits the elite and not the majority of our global family. I know that if we truly wanted to do so, we could solve the problems that keep so many struggling with poverty, that harm our environment beyond regress. But it requires that we choose to do so as a global community.

Tobacco smoking is an epidemic in our world. A little over one billion people are smokers and almost 80% of smokers live in low- and middle-income countries. Addiction to tobacco impacts poverty and development. In poorer countries, up to 30% of income is spent on tobacco, funds which don't go towards nutrition, education and health care.[13] Not only people who smoke (and the families and pets that suffer from secondhand smoke) are negatively impacted by this big business. On many tobacco farms, it is children and the underprivileged that grow, harvest and prepare tobacco plants for cigarette consumption. They are exposed to pesticides and acute nicotine poisoning with long-term and chronic health effects including respiratory problems, cancer, depression and neurologic deficits.[14] Nearly six million people die a year related to tobacco caused illnesses incurring great costs to society as a whole. The business of global tobacco, which is led by six major companies, produces six trillion cigarettes a year, and a profit (2010) of thirty-five billion dollars, more than $1,100 a second.[15]

I want to see global change, but the truth is that I don't have the resilience to take on the world alone. I've resigned myself to small changes like working on myself and within my own community. This book represents my conscious choice to focus on myself, at once and at last, to digest and rewrite my biography as an act of artistic creation. It is also a collaborative effort, celebrating creative women in my community. I consciously breathe in the little joys before they are gone, often mixed with smoke. And I've come to terms with the realization that I'm going to die regardless of whether I smoke or not.

I have found my resounding newness in poetry. The things I have to say, that I want to scream, that you are not ready to hear, are alive in poetry. So I take myself out of the party for awhile, commit myself to the task of writing, with the hope that my attempts at healing and regeneration may succeed and serve others' attempts to do the same.

It's very important that this narrative not be merely an explanation of what has come before, but open to interpretation. You are free to experience apathy at my attempts to provoke sympathy.

As I learned from my sister, what I intend with a poem and its potential interpretations, are not married. Indeed, once Jenna shared what she thought Cigarette Number Seven meant, I was completely surprised and enthralled by the revelation. Her interpretation crafted compassion for things I had not focused on yet inadvertently depicted, and for which I am humbly grateful. I want my poetry to be meaningful to the reader, so that not just poet's meaning lies dead on the page, but reader's meaning makes it live again.

However, I intended to explore with this poem, my being awake to reincarnation. There are things I know about my own past and future, that once I would have screamed into the canyons of my friends' lives. Now, I let them exist in fiction that is not fiction, in poetry that is not only metaphorical. Truth, as I see it, is my prerogative. Interpretation of truth, as you see it, is yours.

13. "Tobacco Statistics & Facts." ASH Action on Smoking Health. N.p., n.d. Web. 7 May 2016. Cited from: <http://www.who.int/mediacentre/factsheets/fs339/en/index.html>

14. "Indonesia: Child Tobacco Workers Suffer as Firms Profit." Human Rights Watch. N.p., 25 May 2016. Web. 28 May 2016.

15. Bowers, Simon. "Global Profits for Tobacco Trade Total $35bn as Smoking Deaths Top 6 Million." The Guardian. Guardian News and Media, 22 Mar. 2012. Web. 28 May 2016.

Waking to Birth, Death and Disease

"Wake me, spurious mechanical mundane terror. A thousand heart-beats before goodbye. A hundred heartbeats, echoing your soul. Two steps to the phone. One incandescent light, lipstick stained cigarette, glowing and discarded."

—*Lipstick Stained*

After my best friend, Tracy, died, l began seeing elderly people differently. l'd lost others throughout the years, both of my grandfathers, and two friends to a heroin overdose, as well as multiple family friends and acquaintances. l'd watched a dear sister-friend suddenly lose her three year-old daughter to viral meningitis, and l secretly mourned that loss with the feel of her daughter's ghost in my peripherals. Over the course of eight years l had five miscarriages, each one a baby l had welcomed and hoped to know. Each death celebrated with silent mourning.

When Tracy died l was asleep, recovering from ear surgery. Before l knew she was dead, she visited me in a dream. We were both floating bodiless in a cloudy whiteness, and l could hear her voice telling me she had to leave, but she wanted me to have something. Then she showed me a turquoise-colored figure eight, the image hovering in and out of focus before me. l remember struggling to understand what it was, and why she was showing it to me.

Waking to check my phone, l discovered several frantic messages from her boyfriend, screaming and crying that Tracy was dead. l couldn't believe it, and the dream was still so vivid. l leapt up, demanding that my teenage son drive me to her house, where l could see her cold body for myself. l lovingly dressed Tracy in her favorite clothes before the mortuary van arrived.

Two weeks later, l remember my happy surprise when her boyfriend handed me a turquoise pendant and matching earrings with the words: "Tracy would want you to have this." l'd never before seen the jewelry, which was packed in a box at the bottom drawer of her dresser. The pendant was shaped like an eight with two blue stones.

For a year and a half after Tracy's death, while l struggled to cope with health and work challenges and to find the energy to live without her, she spoke to me often and clearly. l finally allowed myself to fully believe that these experiences were true events (even if l didn't completely understand their nature), and l accepted my friend's comforting advise and messages as l recovered my health and will to live.

Loss of loved ones is inevitable, whether by betrayal, drifting apart or death. What I realized when Tracy died and I found it almost unbearable to go on living, is that the elderly know loss intimately, and yet continue despite the pain.

Recently, I binge-watched *Call The Midwife*, a PBS series about midwives in an impoverished neighborhood in the East End of London during the late 1950s and early 1960s. Every episode features realistic home births and midwives who help new babies come into the world. I enjoyed the show immensely. It reminded me of my own brief workings with a midwife in Siskiyou county during my teens, and the many births I've witnessed since, as well as the melancholic yet amazing home birth of my son. I also marveled at the show's unapologetic and very realistic depiction of cigarette smoking in clinics, hospitals and birthing homes, even by the doctor character.

In contrast to the symbol of death and disease it is today, smoking was once an acceptable social behavior in the United States. It was a cultural icon of sophistication and glamour.[16] During the first decades of the 20th century, lung cancer was rare. The only real objections to cigarette smoking were moral in nature. Industry marketing and social liberalization led to increased smoking among women in the 1920s. By the 1930s, cigarette smoking had become much more popular among both men and women. During the '30s and '40s, two-thirds of the top fifty box office stars in Hollywood endorsed tobacco brands for advertising purposes—while being paid to do so. The characters and mood depicted by cigarette smoking in movies was a strategic business effort that included crossover advertising for tobacco companies and movie makers. Smoking was completely embedded into the culture of Hollywood.[17]

Beyond the glitz and glamour, cigarettes were definitively linked to lung cancer by the 1950s, and concerns about the health risks of smoking were being studied by doctors and researchers during the 1930s and 1940s, as deaths from lung cancer and lung diseases increased. In the 1950s, creation of filters and low tar cigarettes were the marketed response to the links to lung disease. Despite growing awareness of the dangers of smoking, per capita cigarette consumption rose from 54 cigarettes in 1900 to 4,345 cigarettes in 1963.[18] During this time, there were many strategic misinformation and advertising campaigns by the tobacco industry. Some of the most insidious were campaigns that referenced doctors. The RJ Reynolds Tobacco Company campaign for Camels became famous for its slogan, "More doctors smoke Camels than any other cigarette." Camel cigarettes experienced huge increases in sales for the six years of the campaign.[19]

At age nineteen, shortly after I'd left my boyfriend who abused me, I quit smoking. I had been smoking for seven years, both filtered and unfiltered cigarettes, with a varying rate of consumption from three to ten cigarettes a day. At the same time I quit smoking, I also quit coffee and reduced my sugar intake. I was in a subconscious preparation for becoming a mother.

When I first looked in the eyes of my son's father I heard a bell, and then a voice say, "You will bear this man's son."

I often laugh at the memory of this annunciation, still uncertain of whether it was an angel declaration, or the spirit of my child making sure that I gave him the biological parents he desired. A year and a half later, due in part to my own manipulations, I was married and pregnant.

I know the exact moment my son was conceived. Just a few weeks into my marriage, my husband and I had a terrible fight in which he moved out of our tiny apartment. A couple of days later he returned to get his things and we had make-up sex. As I lay there receiving him, tears falling across my temples, I prayed for a child, a son to be my companion in what I knew would be a lonely and often sad life. I could feel the answer to my prayer take life inside of me. Days later, I was certain I was pregnant, sensitive to minute changes in the tingling of my nipples. Despite our incongruence, my husband and I stayed together because we were going to be parents.

My son's birth was a melancholic and exhausting affair. The night of December 16, 1988, I was kept awake by frequent Braxton-Hicks contractions that precede actual labor. In the morning, I contacted my certified nurse-midwife, and upon examination she encouraged me to stay active and take a long walk to induce full labor. I called my mother, who drove up from San Francisco and spent the 17th doing laundry, shopping and taking a long walk with me through the Sonoma countryside. By six o'clock that night, I was having regular and painful contractions. My husband and his brother (who lived with us) came home from work and quite soon got into an argument with my mother. They left the house. At 9 p.m. the midwife arrived and labor was proceeding, but my husband had not returned. At midnight, he called and gave me an ultimatum. If my mother left, he'd join me for the rest of my labor and the birth or our son. This was one of the most difficult moments of my life. I asked my mother to stay at a friend's house and return later. She was furious that I'd chosen my husband over her, and chose to drive all the way home instead.

Incredibly, my labor completely stopped for almost two hours. I waited for my husband to come home, and showered in the tile stall at the midwife's direction, trying to get labor going again. I remember thinking about the irony of it as the water bathed my swollen belly. My midwife thought the shower would soothe and relax me. It only reminded me of trauma, loneliness and abandonment.

Eventually, the contractions returned and increased in intensity and frequency. I bore the pain with breathing and fortitude. My midwife remarked that I was very quiet in labor and she had expected me to be louder. In the brief breaks between contractions, I wandered my tiny apartment trying to run away from the pain, waiting for it to end. I also wondered where the screams were, wishing I had something that powerful to sustain me through my sadness.

My son, Vincent, was born on December 18, 1988, a rainy winter morning. I remember looking through my bedroom window at the sky's tears as he lay on my chest, one arm weakly cradling him. His father had never come home. I felt alone, abandoned by both my mother and my husband. But I had my little companion.

16. & 17. Howard, M., MD. "Tracing the Cigarette's Path from Sexy to Deadly." Storytelling, Muses, and Rants. N.p., 20 Mar. 2007. Web. 29 May 2016.

18. "Achievements in Public Health, 1900-1999: Tobacco Use -- United States, 1900-1999." Centers for Disease Control and Prevention. Centers for Disease Control and Prevention, 4 Nov. 1999. Web. 29 May 2016. Reported By: Office on Smoking and Health, National Center for Chronic Disease Prevention and Health Promotion, CDC

19. Gardner, Martha N., and Allan M. Brandt. ""The Doctors' Choice Is America's Choice": The Physician in US Cigarette Advertisements, 1930–1953." American Journal of Public Health. © American Journal of Public Health 2006, 2006. Web. 30 May 2016.

Cigarettes and New Friends

"We muse and wonder where the river starts, why the world asks for nothing. You tell me your name. Bonding surprises by the way-side. We find each other, strangers no more."

— *Wanderers By The Wayside*

When Vincent was three and a half years old, l found the courage to leave my husband. l had wanted to leave the emotionally abusive marriage many times before. Life was such a struggle. My husband and l both worked to barely make ends meet. And where l desired enjoyment of the little things, a drive in our new (used) car, or a Sunday afternoon walk, he didn't. Nothing l did was right, and he constantly ridiculed my efforts in the kitchen. l had to have dinner ready for him the moment he got home, even though l also worked all day, and despite the fact that he might arrive home anywhere from 4:30- 6:00. If dinner wasn't cooked to perfection, or was cold, he might spit it out and throw his plate on the floor. l was terribly unhappy and often wanted a cigarette, but l remained smoke free for my newly birthed Vincent, and the fear of what his father might think.

Once, when l told Vincent's father l was leaving, he swore that he'd abduct our baby, move to Mexico and I'd never find them. The moment filled me with par-alyzing dread. Just as in my youth, l didn't have any sanctuary or parental home to run to. l was trapped back in the tile and glass cage where no one could hear me scream. Terrified he would keep his promise and l would lose my child, l stayed. l pretended to love while inside l was screaming. l mediated those screams with inhalations of the sweet scent of baby, focusing on the joy that was my child.

One night, a year and a half later, l had a terrible fight with my husband. Although I'd gone back to school and finished my Associate of Arts degree when Vincent was two years old, l wanted to continue my university education. l tried to explain that this would pave the way for a better life for us. My husband was furious.

"You're a mother now. You need to focus on raising a child," he told me. "l forbid you to go back to school! Give up those dreams."

As l laid beside him that night, l thought about the dreams l had for our son. l wanted Vincent to grow up in a happy home, believing in dreams and excelling his talents, whatever they might be. l realized that l had to pursue my happiness and dreams so that l could be a model for him. His father was a constant complainer, from the moment he woke until the moment he slept. I could see that if Vincent was raised in his father's home he might grow up to be like him, unhappy and resigned to a life without dreams.

When I woke the next morning, I told my husband that it was over, I was leaving him. I told him that if he tried to kidnap my son, I'd spend my life searching for him. I hoped that wouldn't be the price of my decision. I hoped to spend my life pursuing happiness and my dreams, so that my son would believe in such things.

The dreams I sought were rife with challenge and disappointments. Vincent and I were homeless for a short while, carless, jobless and eating from church food pantries for the first year. His father's employer paid for a ruthless lawyer who won half custody for him. I'd never been away from Vincent for a single day, and suddenly, I was without him three days a week. Thankfully this didn't last long, as his father had never been up to the demands of childrearing. After several missed visitations and some violent transfers, I was able to get full custody of my child.

Despite the unforeseen challenges of raising Vincent that first year, there were beautiful moments. One day, an old friend knocked on my door. I opened it to find him smiling with the keys to a car jingling in his hand. He knew I'd been carless for several months and was giving me his Oldsmobile Delta 88. My friend walked and took the bus for almost a year, so that Vincent and I could drive in style. The yellow, velvet seated gas guzzler remains my favorite car ever, and made our lives much better.

On Vincent's fourth birthday the week before Christmas, I heard another knock at our door. It was late at night and I felt sudden anxiety. Who could be knocking so late? I cracked open the door and saw two uniformed police officers standing with a black trash bag full of toys for Vincent. Someone had put us on a list of Toys for Tots. I invited them in as I opened the bag to discover the many gifts, tears falling and words failing. I didn't have a penny for Christmas, but it was rich with celebration.

To be honest single motherhood was difficult and very stressful, but I was much happier. I went back to school, and though I'd spent almost five years smoke free, I began to smoke again. But this time, I didn't start smoking so much from the stress, but rather, as a way to socialize and build new friendships with people at school.

Fortunately, I was studying music. I sang opera and jazz, and smoking negatively affected my singing voice. I had a young child whose health I diligently cared about. These two facts helped me keep my smoking to a minimum for many years. Yet smoking once again played a vital role in my life. It helped me meet new students, asking for a light or a spare cigarette between classes. Smoking was a nice break with musicians at wedding and club gigs. Smoking helped me go without sleep as I worked full-time, went to school full-time and raised my child single handedly.

My second husband and I bonded over cigarettes, coffee and jazz music. We had met over an incongruous cigarette at a choral retreat. He helped me in my music classes, got me hooked on jazz, and we dated off and on for many years before finally getting married. While this relationship had its flaws and eventually failed, it provided my son with a more stable life and sheltered me in a decent friendship, if not love. I had never smoked in the house, but my husband did. I was able to coerce him to accept one smoking room and keep my son from the brunt of second hand smoke. During our marriage, I tried to quit smoking several times, managing a year or more at a time, but always returning to cigarette addiction with a single puff on one of his cigarettes.

The second half of the 20th century, brought about many changes to public policy regarding cigarettes and restrictions placed on tobacco. Reductions in smoking resulted from several factors to include: scientific evidence of tobacco related disease, public dissemination of information, evaluation of prevention and smoking cessation programs, restrictions on advertising, counter advertising and legislation to restrict smoking in public places.[20] In 1969, the surgeon general of the United States released a statement linking cigarette smoking to low birth weight. Under pressure from the public health sector, Congress published the Cigarette Smoking Act which required cigarette manufacturers to place warning labels on tobacco products. In 1970, President Nixon signed legislation officially banning cigarette ads on television and radio.[21] Over time, efforts were made to restrict sales and marketing to adolescents, which also meant no more smoking on airplanes or government work sites. Eventually, varying state by state, smoking bans continued to be rolled out regarding public spaces, and work spaces like restaurants and bars. Even residential areas developed non-smoking policies.

I remember well, when cigarettes were banned in restaurants in California. On the rare occasions my son's father or uncle had him for a visit, my husband and I enjoyed the occasional breakfast or late night coffee at a restaurant. We would sit in the smoking section, and smoke and talk to our hearts content while drinking multiple refills of coffee. It was a difficult transition for us when we could no longer do so. I remember how we complained to each other, feeling as if our joy had unjustly been banned by legislation. Our restaurant meals became less frequent, we'd eat quickly, not really enjoying our food, then cigarettes would be lit the moment we stepped outside.

After we moved to Los Angeles, where my husband pursued a graduate degree in jazz, I became a teacher. I ended my singing dreams for a more stable life and schedule for childrearing. It was incredibly stressful working full-time as a teacher and still going to school. I cared for my son and new husband, and had taken on the care of additional children as a very conscientious teacher.

Once my husband graduated from school, he became listless and unmotivated. While I was working, obtaining two teaching credentials and raising my son, he was home all day watching TV, playing video games, smoking cigarettes and practicing the piano. For most of our marriage he didn't work, as his grandparents paid his portion of the bills. I was certainly resentful, but too busy to engage him in the musical life we'd originally shared, and I felt guilty. I discovered I'd entered another marriage where I wasn't really happy. I'd traded my happiness for safety and stability.

Going to teach often felt like going to war. It was intensely difficult working with children in my emotional and behavioral disorders class, managing the adults who were there to help (but often made my job harder), juggling individual student goals and schedules, all while still going to school. In addition, there were horrible pressures from impossible and ever changing district demands, distressed families, and inexperienced supervisors. Several of my student cases involved drawn out battles navigating special needs rights and school implementation.

While I was committed to collaborative teaching models and integrating my students in general education classes, most teachers were not amenable to the challenge of having my students in their classrooms. Overworked supervisors, who preferred special education classes to proceed quietly and independently in their corner bungalows, resented my advocacy for best practice. All learners have a right to learning alongside typical students, but implementation of this right is often minimal and difficult. A couple of the families I served, brought law suits against the school district, and I was right in the middle with long IEP (Individualized Education Plan) meetings, letter writing and depositions added to my work load. I wasn't in the wrong, but things were tense as I carried on with integrity where the institution would have preferred I follow the party line.

I was in my element as a special education teacher. I channeled all my energy and discontent with injustice into the constructive good works in my grasp. I couldn't do the simple, good-enough job. I had to do the best job possible. I worked hard to apply all I was learning in school and what I'd learned in my empathic life, to supporting behavior growth and academic progress in children who struggled just to face the day. I tried to honor and value their feelings while pushing them through resistance and obstacles to learning positive student behaviors. It was an exhausting endeavor, my sensitive heart crying inside for the struggles my students and their families faced, my dreams full of lessons and problem solving so that I could make things better.

There were many success stories. Children who were suicidal in kindergarten became honor students at preparatory schools. Children who would have tantrums throwing huge metal benches for two hours, responded well to counseling and behavior modification and were successfully integrated into general education classrooms. A two year collaboration with a teacher of a gifted class was filled with mutual learning among adults and children. We showed others how such co-operative teaching could work, and brought amazing arts and sciences events to the entire school.

Early each morning, I'd smoke up before I went to work. Like a marathon runner gorging on carbs, I'd try to compile a nicotine reserve. It was difficult to get a smoke during the school day. Recess and lunch breaks were often filled with escalating children who struggled on the playground with inadequate support and supervision. Teachers would line up at the one copy machine to prepare needed lesson materials. Or break time would disappear while I held fly by meetings with teachers and specialists about children's needs and schedules.

Bladder infections are common among teachers, who sometimes go all day without a bathroom break. I was struggling to pee, to find moments to eat, and often couldn't get the required one hundred feet away from campus to steal a smoke. I also felt shame about being a smoker and a teacher, so I had to walk a bit to find a place where no one on campus could see me smoking. At lunch time, I struggled to choose between a needed cigarette and taking fifteen minutes to eat. But I knew I handled the stresses of my job more calmly and effectively with the nicotine. So cigarettes often won that battle.

I was fascinated and overjoyed one day, when I saw the principal sneaking out for a smoke. I bravely approached her and asked for a light, even though I didn't need one. We had often been on opposite sides of school battles, and I graciously saw this moment as a way for us to connect, not as teacher and supervisor at odds, but as people with a common need. I dare say, despite ongoing conflicts, our shared cigarette habit bonded us and paved the way for mutual respect.

There's something unique about how strangers can bond over a cigarette. We congregate outside the work space, the musical event, the movie theater, leaning against buildings to light our cigarettes against the wind. Sometimes, we're intensely grateful to find a smoker when we're down on our luck and need to bum a smoke or a light. I'm often approached by strangers when I'm smoking out in public, or by homeless people, who ask to buy a cigarette—more often than not I give them a few for free.

In my youthful wandering, I was the one trying to bum a cigarette, too young to purchase my own. Many street people generously gifted me a needed dose of dopamine. I often sat or stood on the streets with these people and talked while we smoked. We became friends. I'd discover that this person all covered in stinky grunge and desolation was a nomadic musician, a once professor, a veteran of war. My compassion was such that I began to seek them out, I'd bring along some oranges or bananas in trade for a cigarette and an engaging talk.

I'll never forget one of my street friends, a tall lanky man with gray hair and radiating creases at the corners of his blue eyes, that made them suns when he laughed. We had a regular date on Tuesday afternoons. We'd meet on Telegraph avenue in Berkeley then walk together to different places—a park, a building ledge—where we would sit with our oranges and cigarettes and watch the world go by. He was always very respectful and I was a good listener. Over the year that I knew him, he began to tell me about the ravages of war, having fought in Vietnam. He eventually shared that he had cancer, which he was sure he'd gotten from a dosing of Agent Orange during the war.

One Easter morning, he showed up at my father's door. He knew where I lived because he'd insisted on walking me home one dark night. In his hands he proffered an Easter surprise, a tiny, live black rabbit, which I named Spider. I used to carry Spider in the wide sleeve of my army jacket while I wandered the streets. One day, Spider disappeared while I was having a cigarette in the shade of a stranger's lawn. My friend disappeared too.

Though I always caution youth to never even try a cigarette, I wouldn't ask for a life without cigarettes. That might mean I'd never have met this sweet old man, or learned the lesson that despite our differences, we are all family.

20. "Achievements in Public Health, 1900-1999: Tobacco Use -- United States, 1900-1999." Centers for Disease Control and Prevention. Centers for Disease Control and Prevention, 4 Nov. 1999. Web. 29 May 2016. Reported By: Office on Smoking and Health, National Center for Chronic Disease Prevention and Health Promotion, CDC

21. "Nixon Signs Legislation Banning Cigarette Ads on TV and Radio." History. com. A&E Television Networks, n.d. Web. 1 June 2016.

Lung Collapse, Suicide and Dancing

"Death on the brain is a hard act to follow. No manner of pleading, crying, believing, or trying, will get me off this train. Only dying. So I smoke a cigarette, another. Finally, I decide to write a list titled: 10 Places to Go Scream."

— 10 Places To Go Scream

When my son, Vincent, was sixteen he had a spontaneous lung collapse. We had just flown to northern California to visit my siblings and were seated in a movie theater when he turned to me and said, "Mom, it feels weird when I breathe."

A couple of years prior, I'd divorced my husband. Vincent and I were on our own. One of the things I did with my new single life was begin salsa dancing. I'd dance 3-5 nights a week, getting to sleep sometimes as late as 3:00 in the morning, then rise at 6 a.m. to go teach. The dancing was as much a claim for joy as it was an expression of a manic phase. It had been proceeded by intense depression after the break up, where I couldn't eat properly for weeks.

I judged the dancing as a mostly positive rebound from the depression. When I was dancing I wasn't smoking, I was building a healthy appetite, and getting the endorphin high that motivates many athletes. I was really happy for the first time in years. I'd always loved to dance when I was younger. I'd been an avid bike rider until my son was born. With parenthood, school and work, my opportunities to exercise were severely reduced. Neither of my husbands had enjoyed dancing, so I'd spent decades without this joy. I knew I was depriving myself of sleep, but the joy of the dance was a euphoric expression of the new life I'd chosen.

Endorphins are chemicals produced by the body when engaged in vigorous exercise, sex, and a slew of other stimuli to include stress, fear and pain. These chemicals originate in various parts of the body, the pituitary gland, the spinal cord, and parts of the brain and nervous system. Endorphins interact with opioid receptors of the brain responsible for blocking pain and controlling emotion. They are the body's own narcotic, stimulating feelings of euphoria likened to the pleasures of morphine.[22]

My dancing euphoria, which felt like a return to the wild and beautiful girl I'd been before rape, soon grew marred by new trauma. Unfortunately, I found myself in a terrible relationship with a certifiable class act narcissist that I had met on the dance floor. Not only did this cause me to feel shame and depression at my return to an unhealthy and abusive relationship, but it triggered my PTSD.

I hated myself, and tried to end the relationship. But he wooed me with romance and attention like I'd never before experienced, alternately harassing me at dance events and in my home. I was paralyzed by my need to be loved, my unsuccessful attempts to heal him of his wounds, my desire to dance and my unwillingness to seek police assistance. I couldn't believe I was a victim again, and I was doing it to myself. To make things worse, he was incredibly controlling and didn't abide my smoking.

One of the inane and frustrating issues in this relationship was the constant arguing. Part of his condition as a narcissist, was that he always had to be right, especially with women. My own tendencies to logic and debate caused him pain and he would make me suffer for it. While everything derailed into argument, a favorite topic of contention was our differing views on a healthy life style. I would say "yoga is good," and he'd go on and on for weeks trying to prove that it isn't. I was having undiagnosed health problems which I treated with food changes and alternative remedies, and he would rage at me for not using traditional doctors.

In contrast to my usual tendency to let the body's natural capacity for healing take its course, that moment in the theater when Vincent told me it felt weird to breathe, I could hear this man's voice in my head, saying, "Go to the hospital, now."

We left the theater in the middle of the movie and drove to an emergency room where the doctor diagnosed Vincent with indigestion. His oxygen levels were fine. His breathing sounded normal. He wasn't in pain. He could only describe a "weird" sensation when he inhaled.

Still, that voice was raging in my head, though I'd thought I ended the relationship a few weeks before the trip. So I listened and pressed the doctor to do a lung X-ray. One nurse was packing us up to leave, when the doctor returned with another nurse, apologetic and hurried. They whisked Vincent to a procedure room where I watched them insert a tube in the side of his chest.

Our little vacation was punctuated by the news that Vincent had a condition where his lungs spontaneously collapsed. We were told that lung collapses could happen any time without identifiable cause, and he was urged not to fly, never to go scuba diving, and to avoid mountain and wilderness treks at high elevations. This was devastating news as Vincent's dreams included worldwide travel. I was incredibly sad for him, and scared by this dangerous threat to my only son, my one companion.

A few days later, we were taking the train home. The lung collapse had been minor and the tissues healed quickly. I tried to cheer up Vincent with talk about how he could take trains almost everywhere, ride on cruise and cargo ships across the oceans and still live the life of travel he desired. But in the silences of watching the world rush by out the window, I thought about that abusive relationship (it would continue to tear me apart for a total three years of cycling crisis and recovery). I thought about how it might have existed for a very important purpose: So we'd have those terrible arguments, and I'd hear his fierce judgmental voice impressed on my brain, urging my son straight to the hospital.

Primary spontaneous pneumothorax is an abnormal accumulation of air in the space between the lungs and the chest cavity. It can result in the partial or complete collapse of a lung and occurs in the absence of lung disease. It is a genetic condition where small sacs of air (blebs) in the lung tissue rupture, causing air to leak into the chest cavity. The causes for rupture are rarely certain, imperceptible until near life-threatening danger, and can occur from changes in air pressure (such as on a plane), heavy lifting, or even a deep breath. Multiple blebs in the lung tissue of affected individuals, can rupture throughout a lifetime.[23] If left untreated, the trapped air can cause a tension pneumothorax which prevents the heart from beating.

Within a year of Vincent's first lung collapse, he had two more. During one incident Vincent was admitted to the ICU. Chest tube, suction and time did not result in the usual healing of the rupture. I'd spent three days sleeping in a chair of his hospital room, and decided to go home for a shower. While having a CT scan, Vincent had a tension pneumothorax. The doctor called me and told me he needed to have emergency lung surgery right away. They scrubbed his lung and ribs, producing a kind of glue reaction that held his lung open against his ribcage. I spent four more days in the hospital with him, sleeping on the floor of his post surgery room, bothering nurses for his lung treatments, and never leaving the hospital until my son was walking out with me. It was terrifying and I was desperate to do everything I could to keep my son alive and well.

While he'd been in the hospital, I'd called family, friends and Vincent's father and ex-stepdad to tell them the news. His ex-stepdad, who had helped raise him for over ten years, refused to visit or even speak to Vincent. His father, living in Arizona (where he'd tried to escape child support payments until I found him) said he was too busy to visit. I told that man that his son might die and he needed to get there. To his credit, he showed up and sat by Vincent's side, crying quietly, then flew home the next day. It was an important moment that sealed their bond and reunited them in a regular friendship and yearly visits.

I also reunited with the narcissist, desperate for attention and love while I tried to stay strong for others. As always, it was a mistake and it was time to quit smoking. But life was stressful. I'd just been through an ordeal where I thought my son might die. My work stresses and health issues were also increasingly difficult. I was still wrapped up in the abusive relationship cycle. Even though I recognized the ameliorating benefits of smoking, I felt guilty smoking, worried about my son's lung health.

I decided to see a doctor for medical assistance to quit smoking. The doctor prescribed me Wellbutrin to help with the symptoms of withdrawal and ongoing cravings. I took it as ordered, quit smoking cold turkey, and got back to work teaching and trying to be a good mother.

Two weeks later, I found myself on the floor of my apartment on a Sunday morning, researching ways to commit suicide on the internet. I wanted something painless, effective, and that would look accidental. I had to be sure that when I was dead, my son could still collect the $20,000 life insurance policy I had. Strewn about me on the floor, were piles of papers I had to correct and lesson planning materials that needed attention. Another pile of bills and household business was overdue. But I was determined that it was all meaningless. I was lonely, exhausted and I hated myself for my poor relationship choices, my lack of friends and familial support, but most of all, my inability to cope with it all... Death would be my way out, my chance to finally rest.

On Monday morning, I was driving to work thinking about cigarettes, how I knew if I just had a cigarette, I'd feel better. Suddenly, it occurred to me, that in all the traumas and difficulties I'd experienced in my life, even with every time I'd felt depressed and hopeless, I'd never seriously contemplated suicide. Now, when my son needed me, I was planning how to do it!

I pulled over and called a nurse hotline at my doctor's office. I explained to the nurse that I thought the medication might be causing me to be suicidal, and that I thought I should stop taking it. She said it would be dangerous to stop taking it, and I should wait until I could see my doctor in three days. I hung up the phone and decided to quit the Wellbutrin right away. I drove to a gas station, bought a pack of cigarettes and had a smoke before heading to work. Within two days of taking myself off Wellbutrin, I was no longer feeling suicidal. I didn't go back to the doctor.

There are many drugs commonly prescribed for smoking cessation, to include two main types: Nicotine Replacement Therapy and medicines that reduce depression and irritability from cigarette withdrawal. NRTs provide doses of nicotine without the other dangerous chemicals found in cigarettes. Methods of NRT delivery include nicotine patches, nicotine gum, nicotine lozenges, nicotine inhalers and nicotine nasal spray. Smokers who quit with NRTs are supposed to gradually lower their use of nicotine while altering their dependence on the habit of smoking.[24]

Now, in the age of the internet and information, a quick look at the WebMD smoking cessation site lists 14 different drugs in varying dosages and methods of delivery. It provides detailed descriptions of use and dosages, side effects, precautions, and user reviews.[25] Two of the most common drugs prescribed to help quitters are bupropion hydrochoride and varenicline. Bupropion hydrochloride is a medicine most often used for depression. Brand names include Zyban and Wellbutrin. Varenicline is a relatively new medicine that is known under the brand name, Chantix. The FDA requires both drugs to have product labeling about their association with behavior changes including hostility, agitation, depressed mood, and suicidal thoughts or actions. Doctors are required to notify patients of these dangers when prescribing them, and patients are warned to stop use of the medication immediately if such symptoms arise.[26]

In my years as an education specialist I learned a lot about the functions of behavior and how to change behavior. The first part of behavior change is to identify the function a behavior serves. Functions of behavior can be grouped in the following four categories: sensory stimulus, escape, attention or tangible reward. The second part of behavior change is to gradually utilize supplemental behaviors that meet the function, but are healthier or more appropriate behaviors.

Nicotine Replacement Therapy helps quitters because it provides the sensory function of nicotine (dopamine production) while altering the method of delivery and dosage. Quitters are given time and needed dopamine support while they learn to alter their habit of lighting up. It's a good model, but many quitters become dependent for lengthy periods of time on the nicotine replacements.

For many smokers who try to quit, the rates of returning to smoking are incredibly high. However, definitions of smoking cessation success vary, so it can be quite difficult to compare methods and find accurate data on how many quitters actually succeed. The US Centers for Disease Control analyzed data from a 2010 National Health Interview Survey (NHIS) that found the following: About 68% of smokers wanted to completely stop smoking. 52% of smokers made a quit attempt in the previous year. 6% of quitters actually succeeded.[27] Traditionally, the first measurement of a successful quit is at four weeks. A study in the UK, found that this period can be used to make predictions about long term success and is also the most consistent opportunity to get information from study participants who often drop out over time.[28] According to Cochrane's Review of Abstracts, about 80% of quitters try to quit on their own with a success rate of 3-5%. Use of NRTs can double that rate.[29] Most resources agree that quitting smoking is difficult and may require several quit attempts.

I've previously quit smoking by simultaneously reducing my cigarette intake and building new habits. Supplemental behaviors have included increased exercise, gum, crunchy snacks, vitamin therapy, singing and planning for how I'll get through a crisis event of high stress, PTSD or depression. I also have to create a definite quit date that I know will be a period of minimal stress. While it's been easier to cut down my smoking when I'm busy working in schools, the stress of quitting invades the classroom. I've usually waited for the winter or summer breaks to quit. Another thing I do is tell my friends and family I'm quitting. Verbalizing the intention and sharing about my progress helps me stay committed. When I make a quit attempt, I cut down smoking, increase new healthy behaviors, and plan for absenting myself from social circles for the first few weeks. This is my preferred method of quitting, and it's worked for periods of several months to years. Yet despite my temporary successes over the years, I've returned to smoking again and again.

To successfully change behavior, new behaviors need to adequately serve the functions of old behaviors. Additionally, behavior change is more successful when there are rewards conducive to motivation through discomfort. Many dieters will motivate themselves with rewards of new clothes and special events to share their success. The rewards of being smoke free are more intrinsic for me. I feel better about myself. My sense of smell and taste delightfully improve. My singing voice has more flexibility and a greater range.

22. Tom Scheve "What are endorphins?" 22 June 2009. HowStuffWorks.com. <http://science.howstuffworks.com/life/endorphins.htm> 1 June 2016

23. "Primary Spontaneous Pneumothorax." Genetics Home Reference. N.p., Nov. 2012. Web. 2 June 2016. Source: U.S. Department of Health & Human Services

24. "Which Quit Smoking Medication Is Right for You?" Smokefree.gov. N.p., n.d. Web. 2 June 2016. <https://smokefree.gov/explore-medications>

25. "Stop Smoking Drugs and Medications." WebMD. N.p., n.d. Web. 2 June 2016. <http://www.webmd.com/drugs/condition-11008-Smoking+Cessation>

26. "Medicines That Can Help You Quit Smoking." Medicines That Can Help You Quit Smoking. N.p., 11 June 2015. Web. 2 June 2016. <http://www.heart.org/HEARTORG/HealthyLiving/QuitSmoking/QuittingSmoking/Medicines-That-Can-Help-You-Quit-Smoking_UCM_307921_Article.jsp>

27. "Quitting Smoking Among Adults—United States, 2001–2010." Centers for Disease Control and Prevention. Centers for Disease Control and Prevention, 11 Nov. 2011. Web. 2 June 2016. <http://www.cdc.gov/tobacco/data_statistics/mmwrs/byyear/2011/mm6044a2/intro.htm>

28. Shahab, L. "Why Use Co-verified 4-week Quit Rates as the Primary Measure of Stop Smoking Service Success?" (2014): n. pag. Web. 2 June 2016. Source: National Centre for Smoking Cessation and Training (NCSCT)

29. "Cochrane." Can NRT Help People Quit Smoking? N.p., 14 Nov. 2012. Web. 4 June 2016. <http://www.cochrane.org/search/site/cigarette%20cessation?f%5B0%5D=bundle%3Areview>

Death of My Mother, A New Writing Life

"The slick flick of a silver lighter, blade Runner style. Bright flame and eyelashes, last cigarettes. Constantine finally quits."

— Last Cigarettes

My mother, whose first cigarette I stole, successfully quit smoking when she was forty. I don't know exactly which method she used. But I remember one of her strategies was collecting her cigarette stubs in a glass jar for two weeks. Once she quit, she kept that jar in view for quite a while.

"I thought you quit smoking," I said referring to the disgusting collection.

"I keep it to remember why," she replied.

About six months after my friend Tracy suddenly died, I received a call from my mother. At the time, I felt intense hatred for her, for all the times I needed her and she wasn't there for me. I was in the anger phase of my grief cycle. I was also really angry at Tracy's mother, blaming her, somehow, for her daughter's death.

When my mother called I was sitting on my patio having a smoke. After the requisite polite chatter, she told me terrible news. My mother had vaginal cancer.

"It's a very aggressive type of cancer," she explained. "No one with this cancer has survived even five years beyond diagnosis. I don't know how much time I really have, but the doctors have given me two to six months to live."

As if talking about the weather, my mother described her treatment plan, calmly answering my questions. There was little pause in our conversation while my mind made several decisive calculations. Despite the rage I felt about Tracy's death that I had transferred to both our mothers, there was no more time for hatred.

I contemplated my mother's courage and positivity. She told me about resetting the date of her coming marriage from one year to the following month. She'd been given a horrible death sentence, but she was determined to live her life fully and joyously as long as she could.

I was equally determined to find joyous moments with her. We made plans for a visit the following weekend and talked happily about her upcoming New Year's Eve wedding.

I wish I could say that my mother's cancer diagnosis helped me quit smoking, but it was quite the opposite. Right before Tracy died, I had quit smoking. Her death was a terrible blow and I started right back up after three weeks smoke free, to cope with feelings of anger and despair. Six months later, when my mother called, I was having one of three daily cigarettes, and I'd planned on quitting again with the coming winter break from school. Instead, I continued smoking to help me cope with the news, and to make the bi-monthly drives to northern California to see my mother as much as possible.

I'd get in the car on Friday afternoon, packed up with clothes, coffee, snacks and bags of correcting and lesson planning (which were my weekend norm). After a long week at work, the drive was exhausting, and I began breaking my rule of never smoking in the car, to keep alert. I'd arrive at my mother's house late Friday night. Then I'd spend a day and a half with her before I headed back down to Los Angeles late Sunday afternoon.

The drive up was usually filled with decompression. I was breaking away from the drudgery and conflicts at my new school. I'd play intense movie soundtracks or salsa music and dance in the car. Alternately, I stuffed myself with sour candies and smoked cigarettes to stay awake.

The drive home was always difficult. Not only did I feel like I hadn't had enough time with my mother, I was usually reeling emotionally from the visit and the stresses of driving back to the job.

I watched her closely, every second become poignant and irreplaceable. The way she shrugged her shoulders and pursed her lips when music was playing, too weak from treatments to dance much, but still full of party. The way she'd get serious about preparing her children for her coming death, gifting us all a Buddhist book about dying. She embraced her new marriage as if each day were her last, with sweet talk, kisses and cuddling in front of the TV. The long hugs goodbye, squished in her waning softness, were punctuated by silly giggles and last words. The cancer would come swiftly to take her the doctors had warned, and I never knew if it was our final visit.

I'd cry most of the six hour drive home. I cried for my mother. For the pain she suffered, for the vibrant powerful woman who was dying too soon. I cried for myself. For how much I hated my job, for all the creative dreams I'd let slip away.

During my mother's last months, we sometimes tried to heal the past discords in our relationship. Early on she said to me, "Doren, if you want to work things out, I want you to feel like we can talk."

"No, Mom," I replied. "I'm good. I just want to enjoy our time together." I really preferred to replace my resentment with love, and to enjoy my mother while I still could.

Over time, however, I discovered I still had a lot of pain about our relationship, about how she hadn't been there for me when I was raped, when I first became a single mother, during health crisis and relationship challenges. I thought that it would be healthy for me to communicate with her about these issues. I might accept her death with less resentment still lodged in my system.

One day, I told her how I still felt a lot of pain about her not protecting me as a young girl. I partially held her to blame for my being raped multiple times, and not being emotionally available to help me through those ordeals.

She grew angry and told me, "Lots of women are raped, Doren. I was raped in a parking lot once. I didn't talk about it. You need to get over it."

I was shocked and hurt by her unwillingness to talk about it. At the same time, I recognized her response as a part of the greater societal problem. We are taught, particularly women, to bear our burdens, cope and go on despite the prevalence of sexual assault and inequality. We are rewarded for not screaming, or told to be strong as if strength is determined by our capacity to bear suffering in silence. Even so, I mourned inside, thinking of my mother being completely unable to go to her own mother for help after being assaulted. I mourned for years harboring resentment, blaming my mother when the real problem of sexual assault is so much bigger than mother and daughter. I mourned for all the women throughout history, that have been owned by their husbands or slavers, relegated to accepting violation as a condition of womanhood, coping with it and somehow going on.

There is nothing quite like death to make us examine the value of the lives we're living. My mother had been a gypsy, moving often, marrying five times, changing jobs and pursuing many entrepreneurial projects throughout her life. She was a poet, had been writing a historical novel about our ancestors' immigration to the United States from Italy, and she had a love of photography. She spent her last year, printing and framing many of her photographs. She wanted to do a gallery show, but couldn't meet that dream. Before she died she did publish a book of photos, poetry quotations and original writing about her beloved Whidbey island.[30] I could see her racing time to complete and leave evidence of her creative life. Watching her eager efforts even in the throws of surgeries, treatments and illness, I realized my own desperate need to be expressed.

One of my all-time favorite memories is dancing with my mother a few months after her cancer diagnosis. We'd gathered at a memorial for my sister's mother-in-law, who had died suddenly from cancer. It was an outdoor celebration, with food, drink and rock 'n roll bands. The beat of the drum vibrated through the deckboards, as I watched my mother shaking her head to the music.

"Would you like to dance?" I asked her, my hand held out to where she sat in a deck chair.

"I'd love to dance with you, Doren!"

We bobbed and weaved with each other, smiling as we danced in the fresh northern California sunshine. We spun and laughed, two beautiful women dancing to remember the beauty of life, dancing to forget.

My mother Tina lived nineteen months from the date of her diagnosis before passing the threshold in 2013. She'd moved to Whidbey, Washington, a beautiful island near Seattle, where she'd gone to die.

The day before the new school year, my sister called while I was preparing my classroom. I'd been planning to start the new year, then head up to Washington the second week to stay with my mother for her last days.

"It's happening," Jenna said. "The doctor said she might not even make it through the night."

I'd thought I'd have more time. I was grateful my mom had lived beyond the original prognosis. But it was happening! She was dying, and it had been over a month since I'd last seen her. I hopped on a plane that afternoon, restless and hopeful that my mother would still be conscious as I crossed on the ferry from Seattle to Whidbey island. The water was calm and dark.

When I arrived, my mother smiled at me and I gratefully lay down on her bed, our bodies pressed as closely together as possible.

"You are the most creative woman I've ever known," she told me. "Be true to yourself. Sing and wear flowers in your hair."

Less than two days later, I washed her body and dressed her in the sarong she had chosen. The cancer had spread from her vagina to every organ. But it was the numerous black tumors in her lungs that killed her.

In November of that same year, I convinced a psychiatrist to get me out of work with a doctor's note. I needed a break. I wasn't coping well with my mother's death, the stresses of the job, and was in an acute episode of PTSD. Sometime prior, during a professional development meeting about harassment in schools, I'd had a terrible reaction to the PowerPoint presentation. It was a photo of hazing, depicting a young man bound to a chair with duck tape, that triggered me. The event precipitated a long and intense series of PTSD episodes. I was paranoid, having difficulty sleeping and suffering from intense flashbacks of being bound and raped. The doctor really didn't need convincing.

After two months off from work, I felt much better. I had even quit smoking. For the first time in my twenty-plus years of smoking, I quit with only one demand on my life: my own wellness. I was also taking a medicinal mood stabilizer, lithium, that helped me pass through withdrawals with the minimum discomfort.

On a follow-up visit, my doctor asked me if I was honestly ready to go back to work. "I'm not ready," I said. "I want to create a different life, one that I know won't be so difficult and dangerous to my stability."

I tried to convince him to designate me temporarily disabled so I could use a two-year temporary disability benefit I had. It would provide a base income for me as I continued my healing and developed creative projects. The school district had harmed me throughout the years with numerous harassments, undue stress and during critical health challenges. I felt I deserved something to mediate all the injustice in my personal life. This time, my doctor couldn't be convinced. I wasn't disabled, even temporarily. It made me angry.

Six weeks later, I was sure that my new life would not be in the classroom full-time, but I determined that I should go back to finish the school year. My sick leave would soon run out. It was the most practical decision, despite my clear knowledge about the stresses I'd face in the hostile environment where teachers were scapegoated for failed institutional problems. My doctor disagreed. While he observed my courage to return to a life I knew would contain many stresses, he argued that I should start creating my new life right away. He asked me to imagine the work I really wanted to be doing.

"Well," I said. "I want to be a writer."

A 2010 Chinese study found evidence that smoking can play an important role in the creative writing process. Heavy smoking can boost concentration and imagination. Two areas of the brain—one in charge of visual data processing and the other determining concentration levels—showed smoother communication among neurons after tobacco was used.[31] Many famous writers have been smokers. George Orwell, Oscar Wilde, John Tolkien, J. K. Rowling, and Mark Twain all wrote books while smoking.[32]

The author character in the 2006 American comedy, *Stranger than Fiction*, is a heavy smoker, whose ashtray overflows with cigarette butts. The surreal interweaving of the writer's words with the real life of her subject remind me of how we create our lives with our own intentions. Her story required that the subject die suddenly and meaninglessly. I often wonder if I'm writing the same story, especially since I smoke too much when I write.

In 2014, I resigned from teaching in the Los Angeles Unified School District after sixteen years of teaching and despite having the most exciting class placement of my career: a group of gifted third graders. Frightened and unsure of how I'd pay the bills, I nevertheless celebrated quitting teaching. I felt as if I'd been released from a long contract working in Hell.

I proceeded to rewrite my life, opening a small after school program at a local church, and writing in the mornings. My life and work were my own, despite the fact that I was incredibly busy navigating the training and business requirements for licensing my program. I woke each morning, ate, took a walk at my own pace, and wrote for a few hours. Then after lunch, I traveled the half mile to work with local children and their families. I held monthly family nights that encouraged language growth, reading, play and social skills. During this time, I completed my first collaborative music video project, a short film promoting organic gardening.[33] I was doing the things I loved, being creative and sharing my educational gifts with children in a manner that didn't disturb my integrity as an educator.

But I wasn't happy. In fact, I felt depressed most of the time. I even began contemplating escape and driving away from it all to live poor and alone in the mountains of my youth. I began researching again, looking for ways to die that were sure and the least painful. It would require that I move to a place by a desolate cold river. I started researching places in Canada, considered an early withdrawal of my entire small retirement benefit, and moving to finish my novel. Once I was done with the novel, I'd take my life, finally released to the long rest I deserve.

One evening, while walking home from the church, I contemplated the discrepancy of my experience. Why did I feel so depressed? Why would I consider suicide when so many things were going so well? My son was healthy and successfully pursuing his scholarly gifts for urban planning and sustainability. I was in love with a good and gentle man who supported my creative efforts. I had my own growing business with more time for writing than I'd ever had before.

I wondered suddenly, if my discontent could be a side effect of the mood stabilizer, lithium, that had helped me quit smoking and which I still took in a small dose each day. I went home, researched the medicine and discovered that it also had side effects associated with depression and suicide. I called my doctor and informed him that I was taking myself off the medicine. He encouraged me to try something new. I had a different idea, however. In two weeks, I was off the lithium and smoking cigarettes once more.

There are many films that feature the insidious addiction to cigarettes and varying attempts by characters to quit smoking. One of my favorites is the 2005 American-German film, *Constantine*, about an occult detective who can perceive half-angels and half-demons in their true form. Damned to Hell for a failed suicide attempt, Constantine exorcises demons back to Hell to earn favor with Heaven. He is a heavy smoker, a cynic despite his revelatory experiences and has terminal lung cancer. There is also a character, Father Hennessey, who drinks alcohol to prevent himself from hearing the spirit world, and eventually dies from alcohol poisoning. Several moments in the film depict Constantine agitated without a light, by an empty pack of cigarettes, or sitting forlornly with the smoke of a cigarette swirling around him.

Both of these characters express my feelings about smoking. Smoking helps me survive as a sensitive in a blaring world. Simultaneously, smoking resigns me to my strange and often troubled biography. Smoking will likely be a cause or contributor to my eventual death. Constantine does give up his cigarette habit for nicotine gum. Will I? Will I find a way to live without cigarettes helping me stay alive? For now, I remain, a delicate flower dying slowly.

The decision to quit smoking, despite the many dangers to my health, is not black and white. It's a smoky gray tornado that carries me away, drops me into imaginary brilliant landscapes, then wraps me again in familiarity and safety. Cigarettes are my happy home.

For me, there is always a price, even as I progress months or years into being smoke free. My ability to cope is compromised, even with the many replacement behaviors and medicines I've tried. My moods fluctuate more rapidly from irritability to sadness. Loved ones, students and even acquaintances will be subject to my tendency to get upset. In these situations, I have to absent myself (which isn't possible in a classroom), walk away and contain my screams in silence, distraction or art. As the world-song fills my sensitive heart with its keening, I find myself in pain. Where cigarettes would provide immediate amelioration of such feelings and allow me to remain integrated with others after a brief break, being smoke-free means either being alone, or subjecting the world to the intensity of my nature and its consequences.

I've tried to harness this enigmatic whirlwind in the power of my pen. I have tried to speak my truth clearly, bluntly, like the sharp tool that I am. People may think that a scream is not constructive, that it is childish, or unsocial, but like the knife, a scream can cut away, or shape and form as it carves. My true voice can be piercing and discomforting to those around me, and has often brought me condemnation and disdain. Nevertheless, I've courageously advocated for justice, wrestled with compassion for others and for myself, and sought ways to live a healthy life. It would be a lie to suggest that cigarettes haven't helped me stay alive. Equally, cigarettes have silenced my screams, hindered my singing, and been a growing burden on my health.

At this time, I have a vague plan for quitting smoking. I'll listen to the book, *The Easy Way to Stop Smoking*, by Allen Carr, that I saw on a Facebook Ellen DeGeneres clip.[34] There are five segments of an audio version of this book that I plan on listening to over a five week period.[35] "The Easy Way to Stop Smoking" method replaces the beliefs that smoking helps one relax, concentrate, lower stress, decrease boredom and provide comfort. **I recognize how altering my beliefs about smoking may be the only successful way to quit**, and this method claims a success rate of 90%! During this five weeks, I'll harness previous knowledge about cutting down and practicing replacement behaviors, particularly dancing and singing. I'm also going to use online visualization and self-hypnosis sessions, such as those provided by Michael Healy.[36]

I look at the endeavor of quitting as being more effective with such a wraparound approach. However, to make this a successful quit, I still have to decide that I truly *want* to quit smoking. I have to set a quit date, and choose additional support services to help me maintain being smoke free.[37]

To be honest, I haven't done any of the above. I haven't altered my beliefs, haven't implemented replacement behaviors, haven't danced or sung, visualized or self-hypnotized. I've smoked. I've smoked while writing and photo-editing, smoked late at night in the surreal of sleep deprivation, in moments of project stress and celebration. I've smoked far too much and my lungs are screaming.

Perhaps this book will mark my release from the smoky screaming storm. Or merely represent a cultivation of compassion. Regardless of my failures or successes, I will continue to apply love and learning to all my humble efforts and life experiences. Change is what comes. For now, I sit unwinding this moment, thinking that I'll wake up tomorrow and choose to sing instead of have a cigarette. Or I may just find one more reason to smoke.

30. Eastman, T. "MY DREAM GOES WANDERING Whidbey Island and the Pacific Northwest Photography by TINA EASTMAN." Blurb. N.p., 2012. Web. 5 June 2016.

31. Chen, S. "Chinese Researchers Discover Why So Many Writers Are Heavy Smokers." South China Morning Post. N.p., 26 Oct. 2014. Web. 4 June 2016.

32. Dijk, J. "Gallery of Famous Smokers." Joops Unique Services. N.p., n.d. Web. 4 June 2016. <http://www.jusonline.nl/>

33. Damico, D. "We've Got Some Gardens to Grow." YouTube. N.p., 2015. Web. 3 June 2016. <https://www.youtube.com/watch?v=0UK-1znL5h0> Doren's You-tube Channel: OneVoiceEchoes

34. Kakosmic. "Ellen DeGeneres Stops Smoking with Allen Carr's Easyway Method." YouTube. YouTube, 2010. Web. 4 June 2016.

35. Carr, Allen. The Easy Way to Stop Smoking. New York: Sterling Pub., 2004. Print.

The Lady Sings

10 Healthy Ways to Scream

1. **Write** - *Write your feelings. Tell your story.* I use poetry to channel my rage and pain. An angry poem harms no one. It is a quiet scream, a creative release. I love to write letters that I never send. I've been thinking about publishing a book titled, "Letters I Never Sent."   Writing my story has been a cathartic adventure. Creating fictional stories is another way I rewrite my world .

2. **Exercise** - *Dance, play tag, ride a bike. Have fun!* I know joy will come when I dance, no matter the terrors of the world. Exercise stimulates the body's endorphin system. Playing with children is like a fountain of youth. Walk on the beach or through the park. Race the elevator up the stairs. Figure out what you love to do, and just do it!

3. **Music** - *Create or listen to music.* When I sing I smoke less. Singing is proven to lower anxiety levels. Be choosey about what you listen to. Music with nature sounds can stimulate beta waves in the brain that produce calm. Gentle rhythmic music can help with focus and productivity. Rock out with music that expresses your angst, but be sure to balance that with music that soothes your soul.

4. **Laughter** - *Cultivate opportunities to laugh.* Laughter seems to be produced via a circuit that runs through several regions of the brain. There are many theories about laughter, but I'm a fan of the relief theory. I use laughter to switch my negative and melancholic tendencies, to release tension and eliminate stress. Watch a funny movie or your favorite comedian. Engage in friendships that make you laugh.

5. **Cheer** - *Be an encourager.* I like to talk myself through things. I cheer myself on when I'm tackling something difficult. I celebrate accomplishment with a whoop and a holler! As a teacher, I always motivated students to cheer for their classmates for both physical and academic activities. We would take cheer breaks throughout the day, make up motivational chants and clap for each other. If you're a sports fan, cheer for your favorite team. When you're watching a movie, cheer for the protagonist, or even the villain! As my mother was fond of saying: Until further notice, celebrate everything!

6. Cry - *It's okay to cry. In fact, it's good for you.* *There's nothing like a good cry to make you feel better. On average, a crying session lasts 6 minutes and people feel less sad and angry after a good cry. I cry when I'm in pain or sad, even angry. One of the terrible things about taking lithium was not being able to cry. I remember when my son graduated from college and everyone else was crying in celebration and wonder. I knew I wanted to cry but I couldn't. It broke my heart. Crying reduces blood pressure and maganese (a mineral which effects mood). Tears remove toxins from the body when under emotional stress. Crying acknowledges our feelings instead of forcing us to forget our humanity.*

7. Talk - *Don't be afraid of self-disclosure. Vent your feelings to someone who will listen.* *Self-disclosure strengthens our social bonds. It helps us process our feelings and thoughts. Talking about yourself activates your brain's intrinsic "reward" pathway, which improves mood, lightens stress, and helps with depression. I have a couple of people in my life that I can say anything to (usually). When I find myself overwhelmed by a tidal wave of anger or sadness, I've learned to reach out to my son or best friend. They know I just need to share, I need to feel heard, no actual screaming necessary. If you don't have that person in your life, then consider a talk therapist, or venting through social media.*

8. Create Art - *Do visual art of some kind. You don't have to be good at it, you just have to be creative.* *Making art improves psychological resilience and promotes functional connectivity in the brain. It takes about 10 minutes of coloring to produce a calming effect. When life is really getting me down, or I feel overwhelming anxiety, I collage. Time disappears and my world focuses on cutting and gluing paper. Art is an active meditation with all the benefits.*

9. Contemplate, Meditate or Pray - *There are many health benefits from these activities, the most important of which is that we breathe.* *I must have contemplation time everyday, and even more so when I'm preoccupied with problems. Learning that I needed time to breathe was an essential understanding when I was a teacher, and eventually led me to walk away from the full-time teaching life. I need time to reflect and process because I feel everything so deeply. Whatever practice speaks to you, make time for it on a regular basis.*

10. Volunteer - *Give your time and talents to your community.* *Volunteering provides an opportunity to solve problems, connect with others and transform our own lives. Volunteering helps me feel better about myself and puts life in a positive perspective. Spend an hour cleaning up litter. Plant a tree. Share some love with dogs in a shelter. Visit people in the hospital. Teach someone something you know.*

Photographers

Judith Foster Thompson

Judith is a Cuban/American. She is currently attending UCLA focused on psychological studies and philosophy. Throughout most of her life her education concentrated on theatre and film, creating a passion for visual story telling. She is the mom of three kind, conscious, free thinkers, Grace 14, Sophia 16, and Ryan 30. Judith's previous venture was the creation and operation of Azul Spa for Women, a full service natural day spa in Berkeley from 1999-2009. Judith is a vegan directed towards ethical and environmental change. She is a non smoker and a lifelong friend of Doren.

All photos were taken digitally with a Panasonic Lumix GX7. Experimentation with light sources, lenses, and angles were individualized for each poem. The shoots were incredibly fluid, all handheld, allowing the models to move and emote. Locations, costumes, and models were orchestrated through Doren, thus creating an artistic triad for her vision.

"I spent a year photographing powerful women. It was pure magic."

Violet Soto

Violet is a Los Angeles photographer and artist. For over six years she has been involved with video & photo productions. Violet draws, paints, and is also a musician. Her creative artistry is imbued with a unique perspective of diverse global inclusion. Violet believes that people can be aware of how smoking is used respectfully, in ceremonies, and medicinally.

Violet shot the first photo shoot of the book with Judith as her model. She also did a beautiful shoot with Liana and Alina at a fountain at University of Southern California (you can see three more of her photos on the marvelous model pages). She used a Canon T3i.

"One of the best parts of this creative endeavor was working with women. The project embraced me, and I embraced it's vision."

Find more on Violet and her work at sotolense.com

Author

Doren Damico

Doren *is an artist, musician, educator and freelance writer based in Los Angeles, California. Her proudest accomplishment in life has been raising Vincent, who is currently pursuing a Master of Science degree in Urban Planning at Columbia University, New York.*

A life-long lover of music, Doren was born again when she discovered jazz and went on to earn her BA in Music with a jazz emphasis from Sonoma State University in 1995. In addition, she holds both general and education specialist credentials from California State University Northridge, and has worked for over 26 years as an educator and consultant.

Doren's passion for words was expressed at an early age through avid reading, and writing poetry and lyrics. She knew she was a science fiction fan when her childhood Star Trek play group wouldn't let her be Spock because she was a girl. Doren vowed then and there, to go where no man has gone before....So...she is writing a metaphysical science fiction series with a female protagonist. Her blog, Many Windows, One Doren, includes Doren's unique perspective on topics such as education, music, poetry and science fiction.

When she isn't immersed in one of her many creative projects, Doren enjoys reading, walking, gardening, dancing, and watching cinematic art.

Judith Foster Thompson   **A Beginning to the End**
Judith resides in Los Angeles with her children. She works part time as an actress, and digital film maker/photographer while attending UCLA's psychology program. She is an Upright Citizens Brigade Alumni and considers Shelton Theater of San Francisco the place where she learned "to not act." She does not smoke, preferring the consequences of a healthy lifestyle. "I value my independence, smoking would be incredibly oppressive for me."

Photo Credit: Violet Soto

Venezia Paola   **Cigarette Number One**
Venezia is a 6th grader in Castaic, CA. She plays the cello and violin, is an avid competitive swimmer, loves to volunteer, acts and models, and wants to become a doctor. Venezia has no desire to smoke cigarettes. Not only does the smoke bother her, but she knows the side effects are not worth the try! She wants youth to avoid negative peer pressure, and never smoke. Smoking isn't cool. It's unattractive and deadly!

Precious (and Mario Ponce)   **Cigarette Number One**
Precious is a blue nose pit bull adopted by Mario. With patience and treats, she's grown tame and confident around people. Precious was on a pilot called "Life on the Leash" and a commercial. She enjoys leash free walks in the back alley and is very playful. Mario and Precious champion respect. "If we show love and respect to all animals and people, we can change the world one dog paw at a time."

Mario works in the dog-eat-dog world of the acting industry. He brings his dog, Precious, on many of his shoots. Mario's entertaining videos of "Cholos Try" show audiences that anyone can do anything they put their minds to. He believes family is the key to success. Mario quit smoking a long time ago. "It's a dirty habit that doesn't appeal to me anymore." Check out the viral videos on his Facebook page: https://m.facebook.com/Cholos-World-Wide-1101276159885259/

Karineh Mahdessian   **Cigarette Number Two**

Karineh is a community social worker interested in people and art. She hosts La Palabra reading series and co-facilitates Las Lunas Locas, a writing group for self-identified womyn. She writes. She loves. She rights. She eats. She rites. She breathes. She grew up with a mother who smokes; therefore Karineh does not.

Skylark Credit: Michael Berckart - *Thank you!*

Liana Cabrera   **Cigarette Number Three**

Liana is a first generation Salvadoreña-Xicana musician, poet and Madre with commUNITY roots in the North-East San Fernando Valley. She strives to live each day ARTfully. Smoking is a recurring habit for me. I find myself smoking in times of sorrow, high stress, anxiety, and deep reflection (these moments tend to happen often as a single mother). Ive always enjoyed smoking and the smell of fresh tobacco burning is soothing to me.

Liana's Tattoo Credit: Heriberto Luna

*Photo Credit: Violet Soto

Alina aka La Bumblebee   **Cigarette Number Three**

Alina is 8 years old and currently in 3rd grade. She loves to read, travel, and dance. Alina doesn't like when people smoke because "it makes them smell bad and eventually get sick."

*Photo Credit: Violet Soto

Kleo Viterelli   **Cigarette Number Four**

Kleo is a musician, artist, baker and health freak from southern California. She has been smoking since since she was twelve. Kleo comes from a long line of chain smoking Italians and she loves it. Smoking has helped her cope with the nagging urge to set everything and everyone on fire, as it is like most things she enjoys, frowned upon by society. Let 'em burn!

Kathy James   **Cigarette Number Five**

Kathy is a mother of five and a Nana of four grandchildren. She works as a senior planner in the manufacturing industry. She has been a Scouter for fifteen years. She is an avid reader, loves nature, animals, hiking, long walks, camping, gardening, volunteering and being creative. Kathy has been a smoker off and on since she was 13. Although she likes to smoke, she does not advocate smoking and would like to quit.

Ana Rosa   **Cigarette Number Six**

Ana is a nature-loving, los angeles native, homebound wanderer, and photographer. She loves to explore California wildlife, hiking and camping with her friends and beloved dog, Chaco. Ana advocates for green spaces in the urban jungle and is motivated by environmental justice and direct action. "Doren's project represents fertile ground for Valley womyn, poets and creatives." Ana awaits a time when smoke is the ceremonial bridge between cultures and not a separation.

Doren Damico   **Cigarette Number Seven**

Doren is a poet, singer, artist, educator and freelance writer based in Los Angeles, California. She has been a smoker off and on since the age of 12. Smoking helps her cope with life's challenges. It has been a window to great conversations. She seeks compassion and advocates non-judgement for self and others. Doren enjoys and celebrates the art of being human.

Nique Haggerty   **Cigarette Number Eight**

Nique is an actress, singer, artist, writer, and model. She has never been a smoker but has many family members who are and understands the difficulties they face when trying to quit and regain their health. She is happy to be a part of this project. You can follow her work on Instagram, Facebook, Youtube, and Imdb; all under Nique Haggerty.

Cassie Jordan **Cigarette Number Nine**

Cassie is an actor, singer, comedienne, dog rescuer & Burlesque Dancer originally from Nashville,TN, based in Los Angeles by way of NYC. Cassie has smoked on & off since college to fit in with the theatre crowd and deal with nerves at Frat parties. She's great at blowing smoke rings. Cassie is a proud, non judgmental lover of life, in awe of God's amazing world. "Much love to Mom, Dad, Jennifer, Shane, Freddy & Sophieanne."

Shakti **Cigarette Number Nine**

Shakti was born in the United States of East Indian origin. She has played music since an early age. She struggled as a child and teenager, feeling like an "ugly duckling" in a highly intellectual family. She sought acceptance for many years but then found it within herself. She is a UC Berkeley graduate and has made peace with her choice to pursue an artistic career. Shakti doesn't smoke but feel free to smoke next to her.

Teresa Mei Chuc **Cigarette Number Ten**

Teresa is a poet, teacher, mother, and volunteer in habitat restoration through the growing and planting of native plants in the local environment. Teresa doesn't smoke or advocate smoking and hopes that all smokers will find the strength to quit. Teresa is the author of two full-length books of poetry, Red Thread and Keeper of the Winds. Her new chapbook of poetry is How One Loses Notes and Sounds (World Palace Press, 2016).

Teresa's Tattoo Credit: Andrew Moore

Grace Foster **Epilogue**

Grace is an arts student, model, vegetarian, and a lover of cats and crafts. Grace is concerned with animal rights and the environment. She thinks smoking stinks, is bad for the environment, and after seeing a smoker's lungs covered in tumors in her science class, she was mortified. She understands smoking is an outlet for certain people, but will ultimately lead to serious health problems.

San Fernando Valley and Los Angeles

Discover amazing scenes featured in the book!

A Beginning to the End

Mission City Church
City of San Fernando, Glen Oaks & Maclay

Cigarette Number One

Ritchie Valens Recreation Center
Pacoima, Paxton & Laurel Canyon Blvd.

Cigarette Number Two

Where the Road Meets the Hills
Castaic, Hasley Canyon Rd. & Del Valle Rd.

Cigarette Number Three

Courtyard Fountain (Across from California Plaza)
Downtown Los Angeles, 4th & N. Grand Ave.

Cigarette Number Four

Leo Carilo State Beach
Malibu, 35000 W. Pacific Coast Hwy.

Cigarette Number Five

San Fernando Mission
Mission Hills, 15151 San Fernando Mission Blvd.

Cigarette Number Six

A Friend's Bathroom
Valencia

Cigarette Number Seven

CSUN Live Oak Hall Stairwell
Lindley Ave. & Matador Walk

Cigarette Number Eight

The Hotel California
Santa Monica, Pacific Terrace & Ocean Ave.

Cigarette Number Nine

Northridge Metrolink Station
Northridge, Wilbur Ave. North of Parthenia

Cigarette Number Ten

Stoney Point Park
Chatsworth, North End of Topanga Canyon Blvd.

Epilogue

Morgan Adams Jr. Sculpture Garden
Downtown Los Angeles, 401 S. Hope St.

Celebrating Friends, Enemies and Strangers

I celebrate family: My mother, Tina Wendt Eastman, whose cigarette I first stole, whose body I dressed in gracious goodbye: Your joyous gypsy spirit continues to be music to my ears and was the impetus for my seeking the writing life. My father, Joel A. Wendt, whose words I inhaled to calm the mighty storm of madness: Your courage to write about what you see and your wisdom have always directed my freedom journey and inspired the honest reflections in this book. All my siblings, both biological and soul-kin, Marc Wendt, Jenna Damico Murphy, Gabriella Grace Wendt, Adam C. Emerson Wendt, Tracy Klane, Echo Hampel, and Judith Foster Thompson. You see through the smoke and mirrors to my true self, and still love me. My son, Vicente O. Arellano, whose life and writing have inspired me to be an author and a better person: Words cannot suffice.

I celebrate the following individuals who without their contributions this book would not have been completed: Tracy Klane, who will always be my truest fan. I miss you and feel you near, whispering over my shoulder as I write every word. Delsy Sandoval, who encouraged me to focus all my efforts on writing what *I* wanted to write. Judy, whose steadfast compassion is a beacon for a better world. You made my photographic visions come true. Jenna: You shouldered many of my wounds and encouraged my creativity through your reading and feedback on the writing of this book. Violet, you are such a creative light in the world! You walked me through this adventure, even up a mountain of ice! Cat Wendt, for your talents, expertise and commitment to empowering women. Alfredo Hidalgo-Guillen: You gave me a writing desk where I could smoke in the shade and listen to bird song.

I celebrate all those who helped with photographs. Scouting Locations: Vicente O. Arellano, Violet, Alfredo, Judy, Ana Rosa. We did good. Marvelous Models: Your beauty and willingness to participate in this project have made it a stunning creation. Special thanks to Michael Berckart (Skylark), and to Mario Ponce aka Scar (pit bull, Precious). You both inspire respect! Photo Editing: Ana Rosa, for introducing me to photoshop and helping me choose photos. Violet for her inspiring photography and help with the book design. Philip Ruiz, for arriving just in time to provide his expertise so I could meet my deadline.

I celebrate all the writers that have taught and entertained me with their books! My writing coach, Andrew McFadyen-Ketchum. Your expertise and encouragement have hopefully made this a good read. My editor for this project, Michael Ray De Los Angeles. Thank you for being the kind of person to whom I could entrust my intimate story. All my sister-writers. You are my sunlight inspiration. Write on!

Thank you Creator. Thank you strange and bittersweet creation! Gratitude to all the people I've shared this life with: the friends, the enemies, the strangers. Without you, my story would be incomplete.

Many Windows, One Doren

Want to connect with me for a real-time eye-opening look into my creative world?

Visit: *www.dorendamico.com*

I curate a spectrum of resources, links and information on the topics of education, science fiction, music and poetry.

Subscribe to my blog, Many Windows, One Doren, for informative and inspiring articles featuring:

- "When You Can't Scream…" Book Tour Events
- Reviews of Los Angeles poets, musicians and artists
- "10 Awesome Books!" Series -reviewing books for youth
- "Masters of Science Fiction Survey" -currently focused on Philip K. Dick
- Updates on all my projects and publications

Coming Soon:

The Unraveler's Star

A metaphysical sci-fi mystery about time traveler, Justice Piper, who travels to a post meteor impact Earth where she discovers a new power.

Dreaming D Enterprises